FINDING PEACE
Within

My Story of Truth and Triumph

STEPHANIE STRICKLAND

Copyright © 2021 Stephanie Strickland
Kekepania LLC

Finding Peace Within: My Story of Truth and Triumph
ISBN: 978-0-578-33425-7

All rights reserved. No part of this book may be reproduced, stored, or transmitted by any means—whether auditory, graphic, mechanical, or electronic—without written permission of both publisher and author, except in the case of brief excerpts used in critical articles and reviews. Unauthorized reproduction of any part of this work is illegal and is punishable by law

Collaborative Writing Support: Sharai Robbin
Edit by: Literary BAE
Cover Design & Layout: Good Ground Literary Services

www.literarybae.com
www.goodgroundlit.com

CONTENTS

Introduction v

Chapter 1   Before the Storm 1

Chapter 2   Young-Lost-Confused 7

Chapter 3   The Perfect Storm 19

Chapter 4   No Fairy Tale 31

Chapter 5   My Reality 43

Chapter 6   Reckless Love 51

Chapter 7   Dejavu 63

Chapter 8   Movie Night 75

Chapter 9   Surrender 85

Chapter 10   Today was the Day 97

Chapter 11   The Whisper 103

Chapter 12   Renovation 111

Chapter 13   This Thing Called Forgiveness 121

Chapter 14   Brand New Me 135

INTRODUCTION

"When you can tell the story and it doesn't bring you any pain, you know you have been healed"

—Iyanla Vanzant

When someone suggested I write a book and tell my story, I quickly said no to the idea. No way am I going to share with the world my secrets and my deepest fears. No way was I going to reveal that the image I presented to the world was fake and a lie. I never wanted anyone to know about my struggles with low self-worth and with no love for self. To the outside world, I was the woman who had it all together. I had a big house, nice cars and the perfect marriage, but what appeared on the surface was far from reality. I had spent years protecting this image the world saw, and that image was important to me. Now I was being asked to remove the façade, and that scared me to death. The fear of people knowing that as a young girl, I had sex, experimented with drugs and alcohol to suppress the unloved and unwanted feelings that were living inside of me eating away at my soul. What would people think of me once they knew about my suicidal thoughts? Everyone knew I had kids, but how were they going to react when they read I became a mother at the age of 14, at 17, again at 21 and that I also had an abortion. I would be sharing with the world secrets I had kept from my family and only just begun to have the courage to talk about with my therapist. I would have to write about the volatile relationship I had with my mother that involved verbal and sometimes physical abuse that left me confused, lost, and feeling unloved. I thought about how this would affect my mother and our relationship now. It wasn't perfect, but at least we could be around each other. I thought about the embarrassment I'd feel knowing that people would read that the man I fell in love with was abusive, controlling, jealous and possessive. That he saw me as his property and used me as his punching bag, and I stayed in this marriage for over 20 years. Everyone would know that my marriage was an illusion and how this relationship left me dry emotionally, physically, and spiritually broken. But the seed had been planted. The more I tried to convince myself that I should not write a book, the more God showed me that I needed to write a book. Every time I would overcome an obstacle, conquer a fear, or show myself some love, I would hear this voice inside me saying, *your story matters*. Still, my fears of everyone knowing my past overwhelmed me. Was I really ready for this? Was I ready to share my deepest secrets? Was I ready to be transparent? Was I ready to be judged? After some long sleepless nights, a lot of praying, meditation and some deep conversations with my therapist, I concluded I was. After years of not knowing my worth, loathing my existence, I had finally found peace with the person I saw in the mirror. It had taken a lot of courage for me to grow up and take self-ownership. I am no longer ashamed of my past. I finally know that I am valuable. It had taken me fifty years to learn that. Through God, and my circle, I have finally learned the greatest lesson in life: I am worthy and my life is significant.

Finding Peace Within is a story about a woman who started out as a confident, free spirited, self-assured little girl, who was curious about life, but whose spirit was broken. I am going to share how I looked to others for love and for my worth. Finally, I will share about the day I found the courage to stand up for myself and take back my life. Leaving a relationship where I was mistreated and devalued.

Finding Peace Within is my story of becoming the strong, fierce, and unapologetic woman whose faith in God is unyielding.

Am I still concerned with what people will think? No. I've spent most of my life worrying about what people think. There is no peace in searching for approval from others. Peace comes from within.

My prayer is that the person reading this book will be inspired and enlightened. I pray that by reading this book, you will be reminded that you are born with everything you need. Your strength and your worth are already inside of you. In the book "A Course in Miracles" by Helen Schulman and William Thetford, it says, "you are the representation of how people should treat you." In other words, the way you treat yourself is how others will treat you.

I hope that this book will help you reconnect with your personal power and love of self, and that you know that you were born perfectly blessed.

CHAPTER 1

BEFORE THE STORM

"Memories are timeless treasures of the heart."

– Unknown

My mother was 17 when she had me and 15 when she had my sister. Still in high school, she lived at home with her mother and her siblings. I don't know much about my dad. I never met him and my mother never talked about him. I was a small baby when my mother took me to live with my great-aunt and uncle in Kansas City, Missouri, so she could finish high school. Some of my most treasured memories were from when I lived with my aunt and uncle at 3609 College.

My aunt and uncle lived in a white two-story house with a huge front porch. We spent a lot of evenings on that porch sitting and talking with each other and the neighbors. When you walked through the front door, you walked into a formal living room where only guests were allowed to sit. The furniture was not covered in plastic, but everything was polished and had a place. Off the living room was a formal dining room where we only ate on special occasions. On the other side of the dining room was a guest room with purple walls and a bed covered with a white and purple bedspread with flowers and sheer purple curtains hung on the window. This was my favorite room. It reminded me of a fancy hotel room. Everything was so pressed and precise. I remember sneaking in there all the time to play with my dolls. Next to this room was an eat-in kitchen where we ate most of our meals and where my aunt would wash and press my hair for Church. There was a radio that sat on a shelf over the sink, and when my aunt was cooking, she would turn it on and we'd sing the country music songs that played through it. My playroom was in the basement. I spent a lot of time down there playing. On the second floor were our bedrooms, and my uncle's office.

My uncle was the senior pastor of our church. He was a tall man who towered over everyone. I remember his hands being big and his voice was deep. His laugh was thunderous and rose from deep in his belly. Everyone loved being around him because he had a way of making you feel special and important. Everyone called him "Preacher", because when he stepped into the pulpit, he preached the word of God like no other could. There were many days I'd sit in my room listening to him typing and preparing for Sunday sermons or Wednesday night Bible study. I'd watch him while he walked back and forth from his bookshelf to his desk, flipping through books and listening to recordings from previous sermons, looking for topics that related to the lesson he was working on. I'd hear him praying and asking God for guidance. I often wondered if I would ever know the Bible like he did. Would I ever know God the way he did? I'd often play church in the basement with my dolls, reading scriptures from the Bible and singing songs I had heard in church.

During the week, my uncle always cooked me breakfast and made my lunch for school. Then we would walk to my school which was around the corner from where we lived. On the way there my uncle always had a joke or a riddle to tell me; he had a great sense of humor. Once we reached the school, he'd bend over and give me a kiss on the forehead and he would say, "Now act like you got some class." That was his way of saying I better not misbehave.

My love for reading came from my uncle. We'd spend hours in his office with him sitting at his desk reading, and me on the floor emerged in books from black history or religion. He taught me to be curious about life, to ask questions and to never stop learning. He'd say to me, "material things can be taken from you," then he'd touch me on my head and say, "but knowledge can't."

Some Saturdays we'd wake up before the sun would rise and go fishing. The day before, we'd dig in the backyard garden for worms. That morning we would pack up the trunk of the Mercury with the fishing rods and a huge tackle box. On the way to the fishing pond, we'd stop at the bait shop to pick up a fish bait he called "The Catchem Bait". This bait stunk up the whole car, but the fish couldn't resist it. At the pond, my uncle would set up and cast his rods into the pond. I wasn't allowed to use a rod, so I'd find a long stick and my uncle would tie some fishing line and a hook to it. I'd grab some worms from the cup and go find a spot to fish. I could hear my uncle yell "watch out for snakes." Later in the day, when we arrived home, we would take everything we caught down to the basement and clean the fish in the sink. After all the fish was cleaned, my aunt would dip it in yellow cornmeal and fry it and serve it with potatoes and onions. We'd spend the rest of the evening sitting at the kitchen table eating fish with hot sauce, white bread and potatoes, listening to country music on the radio, laughing and talking.

During baseball season, I'd sit in the kitchen with my uncle listening to baseball on the radio, eating chili dogs and drinking RC Cola. Sometimes while we listened, my uncle shared stories with me about when he played in the Negro League. I don't remember what position he played, but I do remember how his face lit up when he talked about it.

My uncle was well known all over the city, and he was always being invited to preach at other churches. I'd always asked to go with him. My job was to record his preaching on a cassette recorder. At the church, I'd find a seat up close to the pulpit away from everyone else and I would record the service. Sometimes I became so engulfed in the service, watching my uncle and the reactions of other people that I'd forget to flip the cassette over when it ran out recording only half of the service. My uncle taught the Word so clear and plain that even at a young age I could understand it. He loved God and you could see it. I'd watch as he became so filled with the Holy Spirit, tears would fill his eyes. Before I knew it, tears would be streaming down my face. I didn't understand why, I just knew I wanted to feel what he was feeling. I wanted to be as confident in my faith and one with God as he was.

My aunt was a beautiful, petite woman who hardly wore any makeup at all. Just a little lipstick and sometimes she would paint her nails. I remember she had to slide the seat in the car all the way up to reach the pedals and sit on a pillow to look over the dashboard of the Mercury when she drove. I don't ever remember her raising her voice; she didn't have to. All she had to do was look at me a certain way, and I knew I better straighten up. She was the disciplinarian in the house. When her look wasn't enough, she'd go to her dresser draw and pull out a red belt she kept there or she'd make me go outside and get a switch off one of the bushes in the yard and then she would whoop my tail. She was very comfortable and confident with who she was. She knew her worth and didn't have a problem walking in her greatness. I wanted to be just like her when I grew up. I watched the way she sat and crossed her legs. How she placed her hands on her lap. I'd emulated her all the time. Every morning I watched her get out of bed and get on her knees and pray. Her faith was strong and it couldn't be compromised. She was always singing or humming a spiritual song, and most evenings while we sat on the front porch, she would read her Bible and write notes.

My aunt was a flawless dresser and an amazing seamstress who could sew anything. Every Saturday night, I watched her go through her closet and lay out what she was going to wear on Sunday. Everything had to coordinate: earrings, purse and shoes.

Every year our church held a pastor and wife anniversary, and it was a big deal that lasted all week. Weeks before, all I could hear throughout the house was my aunt's sewing machine. She'd create a different outfit for each night of the celebration.

She was always telling me to sit up tall, and to walk with my head up. If I was misbehaving, my aunt would say, "A young lady can be seen without making a scene," or she would say, "Beauty comes from within, you can't dress up an ugly attitude."

My joy of writing was a gift from her. We were both left-handed and since my aunt knew the challenges of being left-handed, she bought me my first composition book. I had to practice my handwriting daily, she often reminded me, "a person's handwriting is the first thing someone sees, it is an extension of who they are." She was always sharing precious gems with me and even when my little girl brain didn't understand a word she was saying, I listened and took it all in. It was important to her that I knew that I was loved.

We were not rich with money, but our home was rich with love. On Saturday nights, I'd lay at the foot of my aunt and uncle's bed while we watched The Carol Burnett Show and eat ice cream floats. We'd all be laughing so hard that my side would start to hurt.

Every Sunday, my uncle sat downstairs in the living room waiting for me and my aunt to come down for church. As we were coming down the stairs, he'd look at my aunt and say "Honey", that was his nickname for her, "you look beautiful." Even at a young age, I could see the love they had for each other. It was so real and consuming. They loved each other, and they loved me. In my eyes, they were the perfect couple, and we were the perfect family. Our life was simple, but it was fulfilling for me, and it was all I knew.

The memories I have living with my aunt and uncle growing up at 3609 College are the raw materials that helped shape my identity. This is how I imagined that my family would be when I grew up. At a young age, I knew I wanted to marry someone just like my uncle because he adored my aunt and I wanted to marry someone that adored me; flaws and all. We would live in a white house with a big front porch and have a garden in the backyard. It would be a simple life, but it was the life I wanted. I could see it so clearly in my mind and I couldn't wait to grow up and live out my dream life.

CHAPTER 2

YOUNG-LOST-CONFUSED

> "The person who tries to keep everyone happy
> often ends up feeling the loneliest."
>
> – UNKNOWN

At the age of eight or nine, I went to live permanently with my mother and sister in Dallas, Texas. Every summer from as far back as I can remember, I'd spend some part of my summer in Dallas with them, and return to Kansas City once summer was over. But this particular summer, my mother decided it was time for me to stay. We lived in a two-bedroom apartment, and I shared a room with my sister. There were many nights my sister and I stayed up all night in our room playing with Barbie's or just talking about what we wanted to be when we grew up.

Living with my aunt and uncle, I was only allowed to watch certain shows on T.V., like The Walton's, Good Times, The Price is Right and The Carol Burnett Show. I was always in bed by 8pm, except on Saturdays. Now that I was living with my mother and sister, I could pretty much watch whatever I wanted. Every Friday, my sister and I would stay up until midnight so we could watch The Midnight

Special. This show featured singing groups, such as The Commodores and Earth, Wind & Fire. The first time I saw Prince perform was on The Midnight Special. He was wearing a bikini with thigh-high boots. This freaked me out, to see a man dressed this way, and I thought to myself if my aunt knew I was watching this show, she'd have a fit. In my mind, I could see her giving me that look and going to her drawer to get that red belt. Since my mother worked most weekends, we didn't attend church as much as I did in Kansas City. When we did, we went with our grandmother.

When I lived with my aunt and uncle, my uncle walked me to school every morning and when I came home in the afternoon, both of them were there to greet me and my uncle always helped me with my homework. In Dallas, my sister and I were latch key kids. We were responsible for getting ourselves up and ready for school each day, and in the afternoon, we walked home and let ourselves in the house. We were responsible for completing our homework and doing chores around the house, and fixing our dinner. Most times, we were in bed by the time my mother made it home from work. Everything was so different and sometimes I felt overwhelmed and out of place by this new way of life.

My sister was a social butterfly. She was involved in a lot of school activities, volleyball, track and she was on the drill-team. My sister was always concerned about how she looked and she made sure her clothes were in fashion and her hair was always styled in the latest style. I was the typical little sister trying to dress like her and sneaking to wear her clothes, and I'd try to copy her hair styles. I wanted to fit in, and in my mind, if I looked like her, I would. But I was totally different from my sister. I really didn't care much about the latest fashion. Jeans, a t-shirt and running shoes were my favorite attire, and I wore my hair in a ponytail most of the time. As we got older, I'd hang out with my sister and her friends, but I always felt like I didn't fit in at all. While they were all gossiping about boys, all I could think about was the next book I wanted to read. I didn't care much for being in crowds. I liked my space, and I loved my alone time. Going to the library was one of my favorite things to do. I'd spend hours taking books from the shelf, sitting on the floor and reading. Oftentimes my mother would ask, "Why aren't you more like your sister?" She wanted me to be more involved, more social, but that wasn't who I was and the constant comparing of my sister and I made me feel self-conscious about the person I was.

To me, my mother was beautiful, especially when she would fix her hair and put on makeup, but most days, her hair was in a ponytail. She was always wearing this brown and orange work uniform. She had a beautiful smile, but she hardly ever smiled. My mother always seemed frustrated about something. She wore glasses that sat on the bridge of her nose, and she'd always stare at us over the rim of her glasses. My mother was a bit of a procrastinator, so we were always late, which really irritated me.

A few months after living with my mother, I quickly learned that my mother's moods were unpredictable. I never knew what to expect. Some days there was a lot of laughter in the house. We'd go places like to the movies, shopping or the beauty shop. Then, out of nowhere, her mood would change and in her loud and heavy voice, she'd start yelling and screaming and my sister and I wouldn't know why.

I had come from a home where my aunt never raised her voice. My aunt and uncle were strong communicators. My aunt and uncle talked to me about the news and life. They explained to me things I didn't understand about what was going on in the world. I was encouraged to express myself and ask questions. But my mother was the total opposite. She never talked to me about any of those things and whatever she said was final. No explanation. My sister and I didn't have a voice and this confused me.

At times, she could be negative and discouraging with her words. So out of fear of being a victim of her wrath, I became silent. I was no longer this curious little girl who was full of questions and who wanted to know everything about life; I soon found myself missing the openness and communication I once had when I lived in Kansas City.

I didn't understand my mother's unhappiness. I would have done almost anything to make her happy and feel accepted by her. In my mind, I was the source of her unhappiness. So, I strived to get good grades in school and to be more like my sister. I somehow thought doing these things would make her happy. I just wanted peace in the house. I wanted her approval.

Feeling confused, angry and hopeless, I soon gave up and I rebelled. I started lying and looking outside the house for acceptance. I started hanging out with the wrong group and getting into fights. I'd say what I thought my mother wanted to hear because I didn't want to upset her. I knew once she was angry, she could be very cruel with her words, and those words would linger in my mind for days. As we got older my sister was always gone, either attending a school function or spending the night at some friend's house. Eventually, she moved in with her dad and his family until she finished high school. I resented her for moving out and leaving me to deal with our mother and her ever changing personality. I didn't know my dad, so where was I supposed to go. I felt trapped.

I remember one weekend, my mother came into my bedroom and started yelling at me about something she thought I took out of her room. I tried to explain to her that I didn't know what she was talking about, but it didn't matter. She got in my face, yelling at me and calling me a liar.

Then she hit me.

I stood there in shock.

No adult had ever hit me with their bare hands. In that moment, I felt the rage raise up inside of me. I wasn't lying. I had no clue what she was accusing me of. Out of anger, I balled up my fist and when she saw me do that; she hit me again. I just stood there staring at her and the tears started flowing. At that moment, I really wanted to hit her, but I knew it was wrong to feel this way about her. I thought about how my aunt would feel if she knew I was fighting with my mother. We both stood there looking at each other. Then she turned and walked out of the room. Once she left, I fell to the floor, crying. I wanted out of this house. I wanted to get away from her. I was glad once she left for work, I spent the whole day in my room crying to release the anger that was inside of me. I didn't want to fight with my mother. I just wanted her to believe me.

When she came home from work, I kept waiting for her to talk to me about what happened, but she never did. I wasn't brave enough to go to her, so neither one of us ever said anything about what happened that day. I can honestly say on that day I started to feel resentment and contempt towards my mother. From that day on, my only goal was to get out of her house. I never experienced this type of discipline when I lived with my aunt and uncle. I wasn't the perfect kid, but if I did something wrong my aunt and uncle would explain to me why I was being punished. My mother never explained anything. She just yelled and her words stuck to me like glue. They were with me everywhere I went. All I could hear was her heavy voice telling me how messed up I was, and I started to believe those words. Her words caused me to paint this ugly picture of myself. I saw myself as a terrible kid who was a liar and who couldn't do anything right. I felt unworthy and unloved.

The older I got, the more my relationship with my mother became a struggle. We hardly talked to each other. She always seemed upset and angry, so I eventually accepted our relationship for what it was. In public, I pretended like we were this big happy family, but inside I was dying. I knew my mother cared about me, but I sometimes wondered if she ever loved me. My aunt and uncle showed their love by being affectionate through hugs, kisses, and conversations. My mother was the opposite. I yearned for a hug from her. Instead, I felt like a burden to her. I missed my life in Kansas City, but I felt as though I couldn't go back.

When boys started to take notice, I loved the attention, and I gravitated towards it. I liked that they were interested in me and wanted to talk to me. I knew they were only after sex, and I was willing to give them whatever they wanted to feel what I thought was love. No one ever sat me down and explained to me that love of self must come from within and not from others. No one told me that this type of attention was not the way to build my self-worth, and searching for my identity in others would only leave me feeling worthless.

In the eighth grade, I started a relationship with a boy I went to school with. We lived in the same apartment complex and we rode the bus together. Every day before and after school, he would save a seat for me on the bus. He seemed to be interested in me, and I thought he was cute. We soon started having sex most days after school. Not because I wanted to, but because he wanted to, and I wanted to feel loved. After a few months of us being intimate, I realized I was pregnant. I was 14 in the 8th grade, and I was terrified. I didn't know what to do. I didn't have anyone I could talk to. My sister and I weren't exactly close. I felt alone, lost and afraid. Not wanting my mother to find out, I tried to hide my pregnancy as long as I could, wearing big shirts and jackets to cover up the baby growing inside of me. All I could think about was the judgement I would experience from everyone. I knew I wouldn't be able to handle being ridiculed, chastised, and mocked. I knew that deep down inside the things people would say would be a reflection of how I saw myself: a failure, a liar, and unlovable. There were nights I laid in bed thinking of ways to end my life. I knew once my mother discovered my pregnancy, she'd be furious, and I was afraid of what she would do.

I was probably four or five months pregnant before my mother confronted me. I came home from school and she was there waiting. She asked me if I was pregnant, and I said yes. Immediately, in her loud and heavy voice, she started yelling and screaming.

"You have ruined your life! You have become such a burden!"

I felt so ashamed and embarrassed. I just wanted to disappear. I kept waiting for her to hit me, but she never did. A part of me wanted her to. I could have defended myself better with a physical attack. But since her attack was verbal, I just stood there defenseless. She kept asking who the father was. I didn't want to say who the father was, thinking that was my way of protecting him. I figured my life was a mess. No need to ruin his. But my mother was relentless, and she insisted on knowing who it was. Finally, I told her and we went to his house. As I stood beside my mother at his house shaking in fear, she told his mother I was pregnant. The room was silent. After the shock of the news wore off, I remember his mother and my mother talking. On the way home, not a word was spoken between my mother and I. All I could think about was how I couldn't wait for the day to be over. After getting back home, I went straight to my room and stayed there. I couldn't bear to look at my mother in the face.

Once my school knew I was pregnant, they suggested I transfer to a school for pregnant teenage girls. The school counselor said it would be more accommodating, and I agreed. The following Monday, my mother and I went to the school, and I enrolled. It was comforting to be around other girls that were experiencing the same thing I was. The teachers there were very encouraging and inspiring. They would answer our questions and give us advice on what to expect, and they taught us how to care for our babies once they were born. The teachers at the school treated us with respect and didn't fault us for being pregnant at a young age. They cared and they showed a genuine interest in us. They treated us like young women who were becoming mothers. There was no judgement. I looked forward to going to school every day. It soon became my safe haven.

At home, I tried to stay out of my mother's way. Our relationship was already difficult and now that I was pregnant, there was a lot more tension between us. I couldn't let go of the hurtful words she screamed at me when she found out I was pregnant, and every time our eyes would meet all I saw was disappointment. There were some good days where we'd go shopping to buy things for the baby or go out to eat. At times, my mother would ask me questions about how I was feeling, but most of the time she couldn't even look me in the face. I never knew what to expect. I felt as though my pregnancy was the elephant in the room that no one wanted to talk about.

The relationship with my son's father was enduring. My mother was reluctant to let him come around, but she eventually changed her mind. He and I went for walks, and we talked about everything. There was a lot of laughter between us, and I felt loved. Some days, I'd go up to his house and spend time with his family. They always made me feel welcome, and they were excited about the baby. His mother asked about how I was feeling, and she always wanted to feel the baby move.

My first son was born in July 1983, and he was perfect. I was excited and scared at the same time. Here was this tiny little person that needed me. I'd be responsible for this person for the rest of his life. I didn't have a clue how I was going to do it, but I was going to try my best. This was a lot for my 14-year-old mind to process, and as I laid there in the hospital, it was all I thought about. I still had school to finish, and I still had dreams I wanted to accomplish. Holding my son, I started to cry, thinking about how I was going to take care of this person when I couldn't even take care of myself. In my mind I kept hearing the words of my mother, "You have ruined your life." I was proud of my son, and I was proud to be a mother, but parts of me believed her words and I felt like a failure.

Once I was home from the hospital, my relationship with my mother became a continuous struggle. I felt like I could do nothing right in her eyes. She was judgmental, overbearing and always quick to point out everything I was doing wrong. Everything from changing diapers, to making the bottles, to the way I held him. She loved my son, but I felt as though she loathed me. Her constant criticism of my mothering skills was more destructive than constructive, and it fed into my insecurities. I began to feel ill-equipped to be my son's mother. I knew I was a young mother who had a lot to learn, but it would have been nice to hear a word of encouragement from time to time.

That fall I started my freshman year in high school and since I was no longer pregnant, I had to return to my old school. At first, I was excited, but that excitement soon faded away. I quickly realized I was the talk of the school. I was the girl with the baby. A lot of the girls that used to talk to me stopped and started talking about me, and most of the boys only spoke to me because they thought I was easy. I even experienced disapproval from some teachers. One teacher told me my life was over and my counselor made it very clear that I was not allowed to participate in any extra school activities. With all the rejection and opposition I was receiving at school, I soon hated going. I'd cut class whenever I could, or I'd find some excuse not to go.

At home, the war between my mother and my boyfriend's family was fully engaged. There were arguments over visitation, money and what clothes my son should wear. My mother always made it a point to let me know how his family was not doing their part. And then I had to hear from my boyfriend about how my mother's dictatorial attitude was annoying to him and his mother. Their constant arguing overwhelmed me and left me feeling torn. I felt as though I needed to choose a side.

So, I did.

I broke up with my son's father, thinking this would get me some peace at home with my mother. But it didn't. She was unyielding in her pursuit of letting me know her disappointment and dislike for me. I was doing the best I knew how. I was only 15. Everywhere I turned; I was constantly being told how I was a burden and how I ruined my life. Feeling hopeless, worthless, lost, confused, and unloved, I went back into a cycle of self-destruction. Only this time, I started experimenting with alcohol and drugs, which fueled my need to be promiscuous. I yearned to be loved and wanted by someone, anyone. I didn't care who it was. I became ruthless and cold toward everyone; I was disrespectful and I didn't care who I hurt. I was empty on the inside. I didn't care if I lived or died. In my mind, if I was such a failure, my son was better off without me.

I kept this behavior up for the next couple of years. By my senior year in high school, all I focused on was getting high and partying.

My mother and I lived in the same house, but we were strangers. I started seeing my son's father again. I really don't know why a part of me missed him. I felt like he was the only person I could talk to. I thought he really cared about me. I thought he was my soulmate. I soon became pregnant again with our second son. The day I realized I was pregnant again, I cried the whole day. I couldn't believe this was happening again. How could I be so stupid, I thought. My mother was right. I was a disappointment. Once my mother knew I was pregnant again, the small relationship we did have deteriorated. We only talked to each other when we had to.

Since I was still in school, my counselor gave me the option to enroll back in the school for pregnant teenage girls. A part of me felt ashamed to be back at the school, but the other side of me felt relieved to be back in an environment of no judgement. As a senior, I enrolled in an English literature class where I met an amazing teacher. She was an older white lady with blonde hair who always had a pencil stuck behind her ear. The class was small, only about 5 students, so she'd have us sit in a circle and then she'd have us read these amazing short stories from various authors. Once we were done, she'd ask us our opinions about the story. I loved that she wanted to know what we thought and how we felt. This soon became my favorite class.

One day, I was the only person who showed up for class, so instead of following the normal class procedure, we talked about me instead. She wanted to know how I felt about becoming a young mother. I told her this was my second pregnancy, and I waited for her to spill out her judgement, but she never did. I told her about my circumstances, my relationship with my mother, and about how I felt worthless, unloved, and like a failure. As the tears started streaming down my face, I told her how I struggled with thoughts of committing suicide. Again, I waited for her to let out her judgement, but she never did. She just came closer and wiped the tears from my face.

The bell rang ending our class time and before I left to go to my next class, she grabbed my hand and told me, *"You have a purpose, and you are here for a reason."* I thought about what she said for the rest of the day. For so long, I had been telling myself I was a failure, feeling hopeless in life and ready to give up. But on this day, a woman who barely knew me saw something good in me. She had shown me a love I had not seen for a very long time. Our talk reminded me of the talks I used to have with my aunt when I was a little girl. It was genuine and it gave me hope. From that day forward on days when I felt like giving up, I'd tell myself *"You are here for a purpose."* After that day, she assigned the class books to read that would encourage us. Books written by Maya Angelou, Toni Morrison and Alice Walker. She gave the class a journal where we wrote our fears and thoughts and on Fridays, we would discuss what we wrote.

Through those books, she showed all of us in the class that we were worthy and we all had a purpose in this world and needed to believe in ourselves. I tried, but the voices in my head would not let me release the guilt I carried.

My second son was born in December 1986 and he was perfect. A part of me was proud to be a mother again, but the other part of me was worried, scared, and I felt alone. After all, I was 17 with my second child. After his birth, I had all these mixed-up feelings of excitement, embarrassment and shame, so I never went back to school. I was pretty good at telling myself I was useless and worthless. I didn't need to hear it from others. And besides, I was already having a difficult time keeping up academically when my first son was born, so I decided to drop out. Since I was not going back to school, my main priority was to get a job. All I could think about was getting out of my mother's house. I knew if I stayed there any longer, I would grow to despise her more. I knew she was disappointed in me. Each time I walked into the room, the way she looked at me let me know how she felt about me. I felt as though our relationship was unrepairable.

Now, don't get me wrong, I was no angel. But her lack of encouragement didn't help me at all. I was trying hard to figure out life at 17 with two kids. Yes, my mother supported me financially, but what

I really needed was emotional support. I really needed some compassion, some guidance, things my mother was incapable of giving. Our arguments became more frequent and one day after a heated argument between us, caused me to leave the house. I arrived home to find trash bags on the porch filled with my clothes. I quickly loaded the bags of clothes into the car and drove away. I didn't even cry. I just told myself our relationship was done. That night, I stayed with my son's father. When I could not stay there any longer, I stayed with my grandmother and then with different aunts until I moved in with my mother's oldest sister.

I got a job cleaning houses, hoping I would make enough money to get my own place. I didn't like the job, but I felt as though I had no qualifications to do anything else. Each night I'd lay in bed crying about my life. I was 17 with two kids. This was not the fairytale life I dreamed about. My dreams of marrying a man like my uncle, my dreams of becoming an author and writing books, soon faded away. All I could think about was surviving.

In 1987, my son's father decided to join the military, and he wanted us to become a family. For once, I could see a glimpse of the life I dreamed about. I moved in with his family while he left for basic training. In December of that year, he came home for Christmas, and we got married. It was a new beginning, and I was excited. I married my son's father because I thought it was the right thing to do. We had two kids together and I really did love him, and I felt as though he loved me. For once in my life, I didn't feel alone. I didn't feel lost or confused. I told myself I'd work to be the best wife and mother I could. My marriage and my sons would be my main priority. I could hear my English literature teacher saying *"You are here for a purpose."* I was determined not to fail. I was determined to have my fairy tale.

CHAPTER 3

THE PERFECT STORM

"What I do know is sometimes we love the wrong person, and sometimes we marry them."

–Terry McMillan

Shortly after our marriage, my husband, who had 2 months left to complete basic training, returned to the Naval Training Base in Mississippi, while our sons and I stayed in Dallas with family. Once his training was complete, he received orders to relocate to a ship stationed out of San Diego, California. I was ecstatic about the move. I had never been to San Diego, and I thought it would be a new beginning for us as a family. Dallas was filled with my past, a life I wanted to forget. I desperately wanted to escape the shame and failures I had felt in the past.

Before we arrived in San Diego, my husband found a small, one-bedroom apartment for us to live in. The apartment was nothing fancy, but I didn't care; I was just thrilled that we would all be together. We didn't have much money, but we had each other and in my mind, that was all we needed. My husband and I were so young. Not even in our twenties, but we thought we knew everything. In my eyes, we were the perfect couple. We came from the same background; we were both raised by our mothers and neither one of us knew our fathers. I felt as though we were kindred spirits.

In the beginning, our marriage was passionate. My husband was loving, charming, and charismatic. We spent hours talking about our dreams and the things we wanted to accomplish. We would stay up all night talking and laughing about anything and everything. He was an excellent listener, and I told him everything. I shared my soul and all my deepest secrets and never once did I think that he'd use my thoughts, my insecurities, or my dreams to tear me down. We were inseparable, and I was madly in love. Since I didn't know my father, I loved that he wanted to provide for our sons and be a part of our lives. I felt as though I had found the knight and was living in the fairytale I always dreamed about. I soon learned that just because things seemed perfect on the surface didn't mean they were real.

I knew my husband liked to drink. He started drinking at an early age. Before we married, he told me stories about how he would get drunk with his friends and the fun they had. I had even been around him a few times when he was drinking, but I never really saw him drunk until after we married. I was more of a social drinker, only drinking when I was in a group and wanting to fit in. After my marriage, I'd have a few with my husband on the weekends and the next day we'd make jokes and laugh about all the stupid stuff we did the night before. But one weekend I experienced a side of him I had never seen before.

He had come home drunk after spending the whole day out drinking with some guys from his job. When I looked at him, I could no longer see his beautiful hazel green eyes because they had turned cold, black, and filled with rage. I could tell he was irritable because he was acting defensive and argumentative. At that moment, I watched him change from the loving, charismatic man I knew to someone I didn't even recognize. That night we had a huge blowout argument over something I can't even remember. It didn't get physical, but his verbal attack was more powerful than any blow with a fist. To add salt to the wound, he opened with his words; he wanted to have sex. It was awful, and I was relieved when he finally passed out. I laid in bed that night trying to remember what the disagreement was all about.

These weekend episodes became frequent, and after experiencing a few of them, I gave this side of my husband a name. I called this alter ego "Butch". I never knew when "Butch" was going to show up. I just knew when he did, things would become tumultuous and explosive. When "Butch" was around, I'd feel uneasy and anxious, because I never knew what would set him off. It was like being in the perfect storm. Everything was perfect. One minute we'd be laughing and joking and the next minute we were arguing and fighting.

These arguments were intense and heated, like a raging fire out of control. They were scary and they burned. There was a lot of screaming and yelling. He'd get his liquid courage and there was no end to his hostility. I'd tried to calm him down to diffuse the situation, but there was nothing I could do or say that helped. In his drunkenness, he'd tear into my insecurities like a tornado. There was criticism on the way I dressed, the way I wore my hair, how I took care of our home and our sons. He'd compare me to other women, letting me know that he could easily replace me with someone else. His words burned through to my soul, leaving me feeling worthless, simple-minded and unloved.

I felt like a bad wife and a bad mother. I already had a broken spirit when I came into this marriage, now my spirit was just shattered. I felt like his child and not his wife. I soon gave my husband complete control over my thoughts and feelings. All I wanted to do was please him. There were times I wondered why he married me if he saw me this way. I wondered why he stayed if he could do better. I wondered why he even wanted me sexually.

Our sex life was totally based on his feelings and not mine. Having sex with my husband was mentally debilitating. One second, I was being told I was worthless and replaceable. Then in the same breath I was being told I was the love of his life. I thought this was his way of apologizing, but I soon learned this was his way of controlling me. Our arguments soon preoccupied my mind. I'd find myself trying to change to fit into the woman I thought he wanted me to be. I'd changed the way I wore my hair, my makeup and the way I dressed. I wanted to look more like the women he compared me to. I knew I wasn't perfect, but I was a good person and I was determined to be his perfect wife.

The more we argued, the more I struggled with understanding what he expected of me. I kept changing things about myself, only for him to find something else wrong. I tried not to believe the things he said, but it was hard not to. When I looked at myself in the mirror, all I could see were my faults, my flaws, and my failures. I felt deserving of everything my husband said and everything he did. I soon regretted that I shared my shortcomings and deepest secrets with him because he used them to make me feel uncomfortable and dumb. He knew I was remorseful for a lot of the things I did before we married. I shared with him how volatile and complicated my relationship with my mother was and how I yearned for her approval. I soon became afraid to talk or share anything with him. I shared those things with him because he was my husband and I trusted him. It broke my heart that he had taken our intimate talks and used them to hurt me with his verbal assaults.

One night, in a heated argument, he told me that no one loved me but him, and a small part of me believed him because knowing true love had become foreign to me. He knew I would do anything to feel love. He knew I was willing to give up my soul to feel loved. I'd do whatever he wanted to keep the peace. I didn't want "Butch" to show up again; I wanted the man I thought I had married.

One particular weekend, we had plans to hang out with one of my husband's co-worker. I had looked forward to this outing all week. Since the co-worker had a car and we didn't, we were going to hang out all day doing things around the city. I had already asked our neighbor to babysit, so I was ready. Being new to the city and not knowing a lot of people, I was anxious to explore. The day went as I imagined it would, and we explored the whole city. We stopped at the beach, drove through downtown, and we even crossed the border and went into Tijuana. In Tijuana, we stopped to walk around and eat lunch. It was a phenomenal day. Later that evening, when we arrived home, we all sat around laughing and talking about the day we just had. Soon my husband's co-worker left and my husband and I continued talking about the day. I could tell he was drunk, but the day had gone so well, and I wasn't really concerned about "Butch" showing up. We continued to talk a little while longer, then I finally decided to get ready for bed. I went into the bedroom and, as I started to undress, I could hear my husband come into the room behind me. I heard him say that he didn't like that I was so nice to his co-worker, and he felt as though I was flirting with him. I just laughed it off because we both knew this guy was gay, so I just figured he was joking. I continued getting ready for bed. Then he accused me again, and I insisted I wasn't. He walked over to me and pushed me into a corner, called me a liar, and started hitting me in the face and in the head. He had never hit me before. I was blindsided, confused, and pissed. Before I could say a word, he punched me again. This time he didn't stop and his fist kept coming toward my face, so I started fighting back to defend myself. I grabbed his arms and he pushed me on the bed and we started tussling and swinging at each other. My husband was bigger and stronger than me and eventually he overpowered me and I found myself balled up in a corner, covering myself. He kept kicking me and hitting me in the head, calling me a hoe and tramp. I tried to stand back up, but I couldn't. He was all over me. I grabbed a shoe and I started swinging. I must have got in a good swing because, after a few swings, he stopped and walked away. Sitting there in the corner, I couldn't believe what had just happened. I was so full of rage; the tears were flowing and I could taste blood in my mouth. I could feel the adrenaline rushing through my body. I stayed in the corner shaking and staring at the door waiting for him to come back in, but he never did. Once I was calm, I got up and went into the living room where I saw my husband on the couch. He had passed out. I stood in the doorway crying. I was so pissed at my husband but I was extremely upset with myself. I kept thinking, what just happened? Why did this happen? What did I do to deserve this?

I went into the bathroom and looked at my bruises. There were red marks on my arms and a big bruise on my side where he had kicked me. I saw the scratches on my face, and as I continued to look in the mirror, I could see his handprint on my neck where he had grabbed and choked me. I started to cry all over again. How could someone who continually says they love me treat me this way? What had I done to deserve this? Was this my fault? I played the events of that day over and over in my head. I kept asking myself questions. Did I say something? Did I do something? Did I act a certain way to make him feel this way? As I cleaned myself up, I kept reliving what happened in my head over and over again. After I was done, I crawled in the bed and cried myself to sleep.

The next morning, I heard my husband leave for work. Not a word was said between us. Our sons had stayed the night at the babysitter, and I was glad. Once he was gone, I got up, went into the bathroom and looked at my bruises again. I had to go to work, so I began to cover the scratches on my face and the bruises on my neck with makeup. I found a long sleeve shirt to wear to cover the bruises on my arms. Once I was done getting dressed, I looked at myself in the mirror to make sure everything was covered. Standing there alone in our apartment, looking at the mask I had just created, a feeling of shame, embarrassment and unsureness came over me. Was this marriage a mistake? I thought. What's so wrong with me? Why did he hit me? As I walked out of the door of our apartment, I wondered if anyone heard us fighting. I went to work and prayed that no one noticed my bruises or asked me any questions. I stayed really quiet and I kept my distance from coworkers. I worked in retail, so that day I asked to stock shelves and to only work as a cashier if needed. That night when I got home from work, I didn't say a word. I went straight into the kitchen and cooked dinner. I was still extremely upset, but I didn't want to start another fight, so I stayed to myself. I was confused about what happened the night before, and I wanted to talk about it, but I didn't know how. So, I just stayed quiet. That night in bed, my husband pulled me over close to him and held me in his arms. He started to kiss me on my neck. I could tell he want to have sex, but I didn't want to; just his touch made me feel ill. I wanted him to explain his actions. I kept waiting to hear him say how sorry he was, but he never did. Instead, we had sex, and I convinced myself that was his way of saying he was sorry. This was his way of apologizing. At least, that is what I wanted to believe. We never talked about that fight and life went on like it never happened.

After each fight, I'd find myself trying to figure out what I did wrong so I could make sure I never did it again. Sometimes I didn't even know why we were fighting. The smallest things could set him off, like me leaving dishes in the sink. I started to believe that he liked the chaos and looked for reasons to start an argument. After each argument or fight, he always wanted to have sex. Soon my skin would crawl each time he touched me. I couldn't understand how one minute I was his punching bag and a whore, and the next minute he was kissing me and calling me the love of his life. It was like living with two different people. It bothered me that he never felt any remorse. His idea of making things right was to buy back my affection with a gift, and each time I would forgive him.

My husband always felt justified in his actions. Every fight, every argument we had, was always my fault. His warped sense of justifications left me confused. When any of his friends would come over to hang out, I would leave the room so he could not accuse me of flirting with them. I made sure the house was always in order from keeping it clean to keeping my sons in check. All I wanted to do was keep the peace in the house and between us. In my mind, if things were perfect and in place he'd have no reason to become upset. Even though I was doing all of these things, it was never enough. He'd get full of his liquid courage and make sure I knew I was failing. Pointing out my mistakes seemed to be the highlight of his day. His verbal attacks always left me feeling repressed and defeated. I was in this continuous battle, trying to prove myself and my love for him. I stopped talking about my dreams. The only dreams that mattered were his. When he was at home, he was the center of attention.

Four years into our marriage, I found out I was pregnant again. We decided having an abortion was the best thing to do. A decision we both made, but one I regretted. We already had two kids and were barely making ends meet. Most of our fights were over money and having another child would only add more stress to our struggling marriage. The day we went to the clinic, I had so many mixed feelings. I wasn't sure if I wanted to go through with it, but I did. After the procedure, I was quiet in the car on the way home and for the rest of the day. I kept asking myself if I did the right thing. I still carry the guilt of that decision.

Later that year, I became pregnant again. I felt redeemed and that God had given me another chance. I was going to have this baby, so there was no need to discuss anything. This child was meant to be, and I didn't care how my husband felt about it.

My husband's ship was out to sea a lot during my pregnancy, but when he was home, things were calm between us. There were hardly any arguments and there was no fighting at all. One of our favorite things to do was rent movies and order pizza. The whole family would sit around watching movies, eating pizza and popcorn. My husband would still drink every now and then, but there was no sign of his alter ego "Butch". Some nights while we laid in bed, my husband placed his hand on my stomach, waiting for the baby to move. The vibe in the house was untroubled, and I fell in love with my husband all over again.

Before my third child was born, my husband received orders to a new duty station in Corpus Christi, Texas. So that summer, once my oldest son was out of school, we put our two sons on a plane and flew them to Dallas to stay with family. Then my husband and I loaded up the car and drove from California to Texas. It was a long road trip of about 24 hours, but it was a fun trip. We loaded up the car with music we both liked; NWA, for him, Anita Baker for me, and Sade for the both of us. The cooler was filled with water and soda. I was pregnant, so every city we stopped in I wanted to eat, and we did. We drove until we got tired, then we stopped and checked into a hotel for the night. The next day we drove into Dallas and stayed a few days to visit with family, picked up our sons and headed to Corpus Christi.

Once we arrived, we found the base and stayed at the Navy Lodge. The next day, we went out looking for an apartment. I was thrilled to be in a new city. This was a new beginning. We were leaving the drama of San Diego behind us and starting anew. We found an apartment and moved in the next day. The following week, I enrolled my oldest son in school and found a doctor so I could continue my prenatal care. Since my middle son was still too young for school, he would stay home with me. We started to meet people and slowly began to adjust to living in a new city. Corpus Christi was a small town, so it didn't take long for us to learn our way around. I spent most days taking care of the house, while my husband went to work. Life to me seemed perfect. The house was calm, my sons were making friends and there was a lot of laughter between us all. But soon the arguing started. First it was over small things, like dinner not being done when he got home; and our financial situation. Finally, all his verbal attacks focused on my pregnancy and how I had become unattractive to him. Again, after each argument, I'd do whatever it took to make things perfect again. Eventually, he'd find something else and the arguing would start all over.

One day, I overheard him talking to someone on the phone. I heard him bragging about this woman he met and had started a relationship with. I heard him go on and on about how fine and pretty she was. As I listened, I felt my heart breaking into pieces. It seemed like the room was closing in on me and I could hardly breathe. Here

I was pregnant with our third child and he was out having an affair with some woman. I went and stood right in front of him to let him know I'd heard everything he said. He hung up the phone, looked at me and instantly started with the verbal attacks. The first thing out of his month was that he was no longer attracted to the way I looked. He called me fat and worthless.

"I am pregnant," I yelled back, "with our child."

Then he told me he wished he never married me and how I was ruining his life. He made it seem as though it was my fault he was having the affair.

As I stood listening to him, I couldn't believe this was happening. I thought our marriage was progressing, but at that moment I realized it hadn't. He continued with his verbal strikes, each one hitting me like a bolt of lightning, while he made his way to the door. I watched him leave, thinking he's probably going somewhere to drink or to see his girlfriend. I really didn't care. A part of me wished he never came back. I went into our bedroom and shut the door. I didn't want our sons to see me crying. I started to think about leaving, but how could I? Where would I go? I was 21, a high school drop-out, unemployed and pregnant with my third child. He was our sole provider. Going back to my mother's was not an option. Even though our relationship was on better terms, I wasn't about to ask if I could live with her again. Besides, in my mind, leaving my marriage meant I had failed. I could not fail. It was not an option. I started to rationalize what had just happened. I began to tell myself that maybe the affair was my fault. I asked myself if I was doing everything I could to keep him happy. Was I doing everything I could to be attractive in his eyes? My insecurities were all over the place. When he came home later that night, he got in bed and never said a word to me. He got up the next morning and went to work, and I got our son ready for school. We never discussed the fight or the affair. I never really knew if he ended the affair. I never asked. I just knew I wanted my marriage, and I was willing to

FINDING PEACE WITHIN

do whatever it took. So, I suppressed my feelings about the affair and I pretended like it never happened.

That December our third son was born, and in my eyes he was perfect. I loved my sons, I loved my husband, and I loved being married. After the birth of my son, I started running to lose weight. I wanted to look my best for my husband; I wanted to be pleasing to him. I didn't want him going anywhere else to be satisfied. But the more I ran, the more running became about me and not about him. Running became a solace for me. I found unexplainable peace when I ran. It calmed my thoughts and I felt empowered every time I ran further.

Within 6 months, I had lost all my baby weight and I could run ten to twelve miles at ease. I looked great on the outside, but I was still struggling with insecurities on the inside. I wanted to hear my husband tell me how beautiful I looked and how proud he was of me, but he never did. He kept pointing out my flaws. All I could see was disapproval in his eyes on the nights when he came in from drinking. I would tell myself to just leave, but I couldn't. I was so stuck on the abusive behavior of my husband that it was the only place I felt comfortable. I felt deserving of it. So, I stayed on the rollercoaster of constantly defending myself and proving my love.

If I spoke to another man, he would accuse me of flirting. If I looked at another man, I was flirting. If another man spoke to me, I was flirting. This was our marriage. Then, there were times he'd come home and be so gentle and loving. I never knew what to expect. But even with all of this uncertainty, I was still madly in love with him. My husband took excellent care of us, we wanted for nothing material wise. So, I kept telling myself that this is where I am supposed to be and one day he would see that I truly loved him. I believed this with all my heart. I very much wanted his approval.

To the outside world, our marriage was perfect. We had a nice home, drove nice cars and our kids were well behaved. When we were out together, I'd let my husband do all the talking. I never disagreed with him in public, even when I felt he was wrong at times. I always made sure I looked my best at all times. I tried to dress in a way that was pleasing to him. I kept our home spotless. I made sure to portray the image to everyone that we were one, even though we weren't. I kept telling myself that things were not that bad. Because of this, I felt compelled to endure what was going on behind closed doors.

In relationships, there's often an unwritten rule that says we play our assigned roles. In the few years I had been married, I quickly learned my role. My role was to stay silent, obey, and never question my husband. He was the head of the house. I never once considered that his drinking and his out-of-control rage were a problem. I truly believed I was the messed-up person in this relationship. I was the one who needed to change.

My husband reached the end of his fourth tour in Corpus Christi and it was time to transfer to a new duty station. The thought of moving again filled me with extreme joy. A new city, a new group of people who didn't know us. I told myself this would be a new beginning and another chance to create my fairy tale.

CHAPTER 4

NO FAIRY TALE

"Your perception of the world around you is not necessarily the same as what is actually occurring."

–UNKNOWN

After leaving Corpus Christi, we moved to paradise, Honolulu, Hawaii. Just the thought of living in paradise brought pure joy to my soul. I couldn't wait to arrive. I was excited about the move, but I was elated that my sister and her family would be living in Hawaii as well. Once I found out where my husband received orders to, I called my sister to let her know that we were moving to Hawaii. A couple of weeks later, she called to tell me that her husband had also accepted orders to Hawaii. My brother-in-law was in the Marines. My sister and I had drifted apart when she moved out of my mother's house and moved in with her dad's family. After she moved, we rarely saw or talked to each other. I was overjoyed by the thought of us living so close together and our kids being around each other. This was our time to reconnect.

Before our big move, I read everything I could find about Hawaii. I learned about the people, the weather and that Hawaii had several islands. There was Hawaii, which is known as the big island, Maui, Oahu, Kauai, Molokai, Lanai, Niihau and Kahoolawe. We all would be living on the island of Oahu in the city of Honolulu. I found myself daydreaming about all the things I wanted to do with my sons and with my sister and her family once we were all there. I couldn't wait to see the pineapple fields at the Dole Plantation and go to the beach to swim with the fish. The thought of us all being together was intoxicating, and each night I'd fall asleep dreaming about the reunion.

My sons and I flew to Hawaii first, and then my sister and her family arrived about a week after. My husband was set to arrive a month later with his ship. We didn't have a place to live yet, so my sons and I stayed in temporary lodging for about a month. Upon arrival, we wasted no time exploring the island. The more we explored, the more I noticed that Hawaii was filled with a diverse group of people. I met people from Japan, Philippines, Korea, Thailand, and Samoa. We ate poke, which is raw tuna or salmon served with poke seasoning. We ate poi, which is a native cuisine of Hawaii, Korean barbecue, fried rice and my favorite pancit, which is fried noodles cooked with chopped vegetables.

Once our month was up, before my husband arrived, we were offered housing by the military. The housing I accepted was located inside of a crater, a dead volcano. To get to our house, you had to drive down into a huge crater to see the housing units. My sons thought it was pretty cool, and I was in total awe. Everything inside the crater was green, and there were vibrant wildflowers everywhere. Our house was the typical base housing, a two-story townhouse. Downstairs there was a kitchen, a huge living room and a half-bath. Upstairs, there were four bedrooms and two bathrooms. My sons quickly ran upstairs to pick out their rooms.

A few days later, the military delivered our furniture and I began to unpack, getting the house ready in anticipation of my husband's arrival. I loved living in Hawaii. Every day, the weather was perfect. It never got over 80 degrees, and there was always a light breeze. It was the perfect running weather. Sometimes on my run it would start misting outside and the wetness hitting my skin cooled me off. It felt so soothing to my skin. Everywhere we went, the people were friendly and everyone was laid back. There was no rush for anything.

The ship my husband would arrive on would be stationed at Pearl Harbor Naval Base in the city of Honolulu. My brother-in-law, who was in the marines, would be stationed at Kaneohe Marine Base in Kaneohe, which was located on the north shore of Oahu. The very first time I drove to visit my sister, I thought I was lost and my sons kept asking if we were there yet. To get to the North shore, I had to drive through a long dark tunnel, which ran through a mountain. As we kept going higher and higher, my heart began to sink into my chest. How much longer, I thought. Once I came to the end of this tunnel, I drove out to a picturesque view I will never forget. The view literally took my breath away. The water was crystal clear and it looked like it stretched to infinity and beyond. There was green foliage and colorful flowers everywhere. Tall palm trees and banana plants filled the sky and they went on for miles. In between all of this magnificent landscape, I could see houses where people lived. I rolled down the window in the car and I felt a gentle breeze hit my face. At that moment, I fell in love with Hawaii, and I wanted to stay there forever.

A month later, my husband's ship was to arrive. A week before the ship was to pull in, I went out and bought the perfect outfit. The day before, I had my hair and my nails done. I wanted to look my best. The night before, I laid out the sexiest lingerie I had. I wanted everything to be perfect. My sister and her husband agreed to watch our sons and host a barbeque at their house, so I didn't have to worry about cooking a meal. All I had to do was make sure the house was clean and the car was washed. The night before he arrived, I couldn't sleep. I tossed and turned, trying to imagine how I would feel when I saw him. Would I be filled with excitement? Or would I be filled with the uneasy anxiety always felt when I was around him? I laid in bed all night thinking about our reunion. The next day, I woke up super early, got dressed and hurried to the pier so I could see the ship when it pulled in. I stood there on the pier with all the other wives waiting for the ship's arrival. As the ship pulled into the pier, I could feel the excitement amongst us all. Some women were crying, some were screaming and jumping up and down. I just stood there, still unsure of what to expect. I hope he liked my dress and my hair was all I kept thinking. Once our eyes met, I waited for his response. Once I saw him smile, I smiled and I walked over and gave him a kiss. He was excited to see me, and I felt relieved. As the distressed feelings left my body, I couldn't wait to get him home. At home, I gave him a quick tour of the house, making the last room our bedroom. In our bedroom, he grabbed me and threw me on the bed. We spent most of the day getting reacquainted. There was a lot of sex and a lot of talking and laughter. It reminded me of when we were first married, when I felt safe and loved. Laying there next to him, I saw the man I fell in love with. I hadn't felt this way with him in a long time. Later that evening, we drove out to my sister's house to eat and to pick up our sons. The day was perfect. Just like I imagined it would be.

The first six months after my husband arrived home were delightful. We were living the life I dreamed about, the fairytale. There was a lot of laughter in the house, a lot of deep conversations between us and a lot of love making. Things were good. We spent time exploring the island, hosting cookouts, and visiting with my sister and her family. I woke up each day feeling at peace and so in love. But gradually, without warning, the honeymoon phase was over and that peace I once had slowly diminished. I realized that living in paradise was not going to change the problems in my marriage. Before long, my husband's alter ego "Butch" started showing up and the fairytale was no more. The fighting and arguing began. First it was over money. We argued that I was not helping enough with the finances. I already knew I needed to find a job, and I was waiting until we were settled before I started looking. To calm the chaos, and to please my husband, I changed my focus and finding a job became my main priority. After a couple of months of applying at various places, I was hired at the Navy Exchange, a military retail store. I worked in the cash cage as a cashier balancing the credit card receipts, cash from the cash registers and vending machines. The hours were not great. Most days I worked from 5am to 1pm and most weekends and holidays. When he could no longer moan and grumble about me not working, his focus turned toward my work hours. To appease him and to once again calm his continuous uproar, I found another job as a cash teller at a credit union. This job was less money, but it came with set hours: Monday to Friday, 9 to 5 and no weekends. In my mind, this was perfect. I wondered what he could find wrong.

I just knew this would calm the uneasy tension between us and we could go back to living our fairytale. This did calm things down for a while, but when he could no longer find fault in my job, my husband redirected his focus on anything that would tear me down. He'd critique the way I dressed. I didn't dress like the other wives. I was too fat. When I started losing weight, I was too skinny. He'd criticized the way I kept the house. It wasn't clean enough. Then there were the backhanded remarks. Sometimes I'd hear him singing, "My momma told me, you better shop around." I felt as though he was implying that he could do better. When I brought this to his attention, he just laughed, saying it was just a song.

Then there were nights he'd come home drunk from being out with his friends and as soon as he entered the house, the belittlement started. Those were the nights he'd let me know he should have never married me. In his rants he let me know he could have easily married someone more attractive and enticing than me. Someone who was better in bed. I was an ungrateful bitch who didn't appreciate him and everything he had done for our family.

Even though everything inside of me wanted to defend myself, I knew not to say a word. I had learned my role in this marriage and that was to stay silent. I didn't want to fight. I told myself it was better to endure his verbal abuse and not provoke the physical abuse. So, I would sit there taking it all in. Purposely holding my breath to prevent myself from saying everything I felt. I saw the sacrifices he made daily for us: being gone all the time, working long hours. I loved him for it. I thought I was showing my appreciation by doing everything I could to satisfy him in every way. But "Butch" made it clear that I was failing. He made it clear our marriage was no fairytale.

I'd sit in silence, feeling no emotion and looking helpless with a blank look on my face. His words cut through me like a sword and with each cut, I could feel the little self-worth I had, slowly draining away. I didn't know what else to do or what else to say. I didn't know how to reassure him that he wasn't alone and that we were in this together. I just didn't know what to do. After he was done with the verbal abuse, he always wanted to have sex. Having sex with him while he was drunk was the last thing I wanted to do. Feeling his touch, and the smell on his breath made me sick. My whole body would tighten up and I'd want to vomit. But I would comply because I knew if I didn't things would get physical, and I just wanted the night to end. I wanted him to go to sleep, so I could find peace in the silence.

His drunken rants always left me depleted. After each attack, I'd lay in bed the next day trying to figure out what I did and what I needed to do so it would not happen again. I'd tell myself he was drunk and it was the alcohol talking. I'd convince myself that he didn't mean the things he said. But the more the episodes occurred, the harder it was for me to shake off the condemnation I felt towards myself. I felt so useless, undesirable and like a failure. To compensate for those feelings, I'd go on these relentless missions to prove my love for him. I was determined to show him I could be the woman he wanted me to be. I yearned for his approval. In my mind, I needed his approval to feel worthy. I constantly worried about my weight and worried about how I dressed and how I looked. I second guessed my thoughts. I just knew my insecurities were the cause of his unhappiness with me. I felt as though I was the one keeping us from living the fairytale.

It was a holiday weekend and my sister invited us over to her home for a barbeque. We spent the day playing volleyball, swimming and running through the sprinklers. Once it got dark, we all went inside to chill. The kids were playing upstairs, while the adults were downstairs, about to be busy playing cards at the kitchen table. All of a sudden, we heard police sirens outside. There seemed to be something going on, so all the adults went outside to see. When we looked we saw there were a couple of police cars parked outside in front of a house a few doors down from my sister's, and the police were talking to someone on the front lawn. We really couldn't tell what was going on, and after a few minutes of being nosey, we all decided to head back into the house. Me, my sister and her husband all went in and sat back down at the kitchen table. I thought my husband was right behind us, but he wasn't. We all just thought he was in the restroom, so we continued to talk while we waited.

After a few minutes, I went and knocked on the restroom door and I realized he wasn't in there. We all soon realized that he wasn't anywhere in the house, and he had taken the car. At first I thought maybe he went to get some more cigarettes or some more beer. So, we waited for him to come back. About fifteen minutes later, when he didn't come back, I started to worry. I could tell my sister and my brother-in-law were becoming irritated, and so was I.

My sister started asking me where he went, but I didn't know. As I sat there, trying to figure out where he could have gone, I started to feel my body tense up and I felt uneasy. The last thing I wanted my sister and her husband to see was "Butch". My husband had been drinking that day with my brother-in-law, but I wasn't worried because my husband never showed "Butch" in public only behind closed doors.

I kept walking outside, hoping that he'd drive back up. Where did he go? I waited a few more minutes and I started calling home to see if he was there. After a few calls to our house, he finally answered the phone. I asked him what was wrong with him and why he left. He told me to come home so we could talk. I asked him how, since he had taken the car. There was a long silence, so I hung up the phone. I took a long breath in disgust, thinking about what the problem could be, and how I was going to explain this to everyone. I took another long, deep breath and asked my sister if she could give me a ride home. Again, she asked me why he left, and I quietly said I didn't know because I never knew what triggered "Butch". The whole way to our house I kept wondering what had I done to upset him? We were all having a good time and he had to go and ruin it. I was pissed.

When I got home, I sent our sons straight to bed. My husband was sitting in the den. I slowly walked into the den, preparing myself for the attack. I asked him again, why did he leave. He looked at me and asked if I was having sex with my sister's husband. I asked who and he yelled, "with your sister's husband." I told him no. I couldn't believe he was accusing me of having sex with my brother-in-law. I became infuriated, and I started shaking with anger. I wanted to punch him in his face. I yelled at my husband, "He is family!" He hollered back that he knew I was a slut, but had married me anyway. "Butch" got up in my face and yelled that the two of us were flirting with each other at the table right in front of him. He said that I called my brother-in-law "babe". The glass he had in his hand, he took it and threw it at the wall and in that instant, I knew tonight would not be a night of a verbal attack. We were going to fight.

Before I could say a word, he came towards me, grabbed my neck and pushed me into the wall. I could feel the pressure around my neck, and when I looked him in the eyes, I could see his rage. I tried to remove his hands from my neck, but with each attempt, his grip got tighter. Then, all of a sudden, when he could feel my body becoming limp he let go and walked away.

As I fought to regain my breath, I stood there confused and in rage. I thought, why didn't he ask me this when we were at my sister's house? We could have straightened this out there. I considered my sister's husband as my brother. He called me sis. He came over to the house all the time to hang out with my husband and our sons. I stood there against the wall wanting to fight back but afraid; I knew that would only make things worse, so I did nothing. I just stood there frozen with anger and feeling helpless, with tears streaming down my face. I grabbed the phone and called my sister, not for her to come and get me, but to prove my husband wrong.

First, my sister tried to assure him that he was wrong, then my brother-in-law got on the phone and tried to calm him down, but no one could change his mind. In that moment of mayhem, some part of me believed he intentionally caused this confusion to isolate me from my sister. He knew how much I wanted to reconnect with her because it was all I talked about. He knew his actions would humiliate me and I would not know how to face her after that night. I had not shared with my sister or anyone about the abuse I had been enduring in my marriage. It was my secret, and I never wanted anyone to know about this part of my life.

Weeks went by before I saw my sister again, and when I did, I felt the awkwardness between us. Nothing was said about what happened that night, I just noticed there were not many family gatherings when my husband was home. I mostly saw my sister and her family when he was out to sea. After a year, my sister left Hawaii and moved back to Texas. On the day she was flying out, I went to the airport to see her off. I felt really bad that we didn't reconnect the way I wanted to. It bothered me that I had allowed my husband's insecurities and his need to have control, interfere with us rebuilding our relationship.

The ship my husband was on was a new ship and the crew spent a lot of time out at sea testing the mechanics. There would be times he would be gone for six months straight. I have to admit, at times, I was glad when the ship was gone, because I knew there would be peace in the house. It was like my sons and I could breathe. On Friday evenings, we would go to the drive-in or explore the island. I got to know some of the other military wives that lived on our street, and we all agreed that we'd look out for each other while our husbands were out to sea. Some nights when I arrived home from work, one of the wives would have already fed my sons dinner and made sure their homework was done. My house was the hang out house. My sons always invited their friends over to spend the night. I'd make them pallets out of blankets on the floor in the den and we stayed up all night watching movies and eating pizza. Some nights, me and some of the other wives would go out to eat and go dancing. I really enjoyed those nights. They were freeing. We'd find a place where we could sit outside and feel the ocean breeze while we ate our dinner. We'd talked about anything and everything that came to our minds. We talked about our dreams, our goals, our fantasies. And after a couple of glasses of wine, we all had advice on life and sex. When the wives started to talk about their marriages, I just sat and listened. I had no advice to give. I was too ashamed to talk about the problems in my marriage. I never wanted anyone to know about the turmoil I was experiencing.

My husband and I communicated by writing letters to each other when he was out at sea. In those letters, we'd share our day-to-day lives. He'd tell me about all the places the ship was visiting. I'd let him know about our sons and what we had been up to. In his letters, he expressed how much he loved me. He shared that I was the love of his life. He'd let me know that he couldn't wait to feel me and hold me in his arms. When I would read those letters, I'd tell myself this is the man I fell in love with. I often wondered why I only saw a glimpse of this man when he was at home. I wondered if it was my fault that "Butch" kept appearing in my marriage. In my letters, I expressed to him how much I really loved him and missed him. Sometimes in my letters, I'd include quotes from poetry or lyrics from a song that expressed the way I felt about him and about us. I'd make sure to share with him my desires for us and our family. I really wanted us to be together forever.

This would go on for months while he was gone, and with each letter, I found myself falling in love with him all over again. Each time the ship would pull in from being out to sea, it was like a new beginning and a chance for us to get the fairy tale right. There was always a cookout planned the first weekend after the ship pulled into port from a deployment. All the families would gather together at someone's house and we'd spend the day enjoying each other's company.

I loved it when it was our turn to host the cookout at our house. The house would be filled with laughter. All the men would be sitting around the table playing cards or dominos drinking beer. All the women would be busy in the kitchen helping each other cook, telling stories and taking turns watching the kids. I loved the vibe I felt throughout the house. It was so intoxicating, like the high I felt after a long run, and I didn't want it to end. I'd look over at my husband, he'd look up at me and we both would smile. The perfect ending to the perfect day, like a fairy tale.

But just as soon as I thought we were on one accord, things would always change. It would be subtle at first. It would always start out with him comparing me to other women. Or he'd belittle my job by saying my job wasn't important. Then there was that stupid song he kept singing over and over, "My momma told me, you better shop around."

I knew he was implying that he could do better. His actions bewildered me, and I wanted to know why he could be so heartless. When I questioned him about why he was always singing that song, his response was he was just joking and he didn't mean it. Bullshit! He was intentional, and he knew his actions would upset me. Each time I heard him singing that song, my body would tense up and instead of saying something and starting an argument, I'd hold in my anger, withdraw inward and start counting down the days until he left.

One evening, he came home from being out with his friends, and we got into a disagreement over how to discipline one of our sons. The argument started downstairs, with us arguing back and forth. Then, as my husband started going upstairs, I followed him, continuing to talk and letting him know that I didn't agree with him. We were almost at the top of the stairs when he turned around and grabbed me around the neck and carried me up the rest of the stairs. I could feel him squeezing my neck tighter and tighter, taking my breath away.

I tried to pull his hand from around my neck, but I couldn't. In our room, he threw me into the wall and told me not to question him. Then he walked away. My body hit the wall and I fell to the floor. I balled myself up in the corner, waiting for him to come back. I felt the rage raising up inside me like boiling water. I was more upset with myself than I was with him.

Normally, when he went on his drinking rants, I stayed quiet and let him talk until he got tired, hoping that he'd just pass out. But this time I didn't. This time, I spoke up and argued back. Sitting there on the floor, I told myself I should have stayed quiet. What did my speaking up accomplish? Our sons were downstairs watching T.V. and heard everything. Being too ashamed to go back downstairs, I stayed in our bedroom for the rest of the night. That night when he came to bed, I knew he wanted to have sex. He pulled me close and began to whisper how much he loved me. I heard him whisper to me that if I loved him, I needed to obey and not challenge him. I just laid there unresponsive. I could smell the liquor on him, and I wanted to vomit. I wanted to fight him off, but I knew that would just prolong the night. I just wanted him to hurry up and get it over with. So, I just laid there, and I wondered if he noticed the handprint he left on my neck. I wondered if he had any remorse at all.

After he finished, he rolled over and fell asleep, and I went and took a shower and cried. The next day we both woke up and went about our day as if the night before never happened. There was no apology from him, which left me conflicted and trying to understand why he treated me this way, and why I was okay with it. Why couldn't I see my worth?

CHAPTER 5

MY REALITY

"Hardest reality is accepting the reality."

—JOKER

In October 1999, we left the beautiful island of Hawaii for Great Lakes, Illinois. A new place, a new beginning. With each move I felt as though it was a new start for us, a chance to live the fairy tale. Upon our arrival in Great Lakes, I noticed how old the city looked. It was gloomy and dirty and I thought to myself, "I left paradise for this place?". We stayed in a hotel over the weekend and that Monday we were offered military housing. The house we moved into was five minutes from the military base where my husband was stationed. Around our house and the base were a lot of abandoned buildings and run-down homes. It was very depressing. All I kept thinking about was that I left Hawaii to come here. Shortly after we arrived, there was a major snowstorm and snow was everywhere. The snow was so pretty. It was pure white and beautiful. On the first day, the whole family, including the dogs, couldn't wait to go outside and play in it. We spent the whole day building snowmen and having snowball fights. But after a month, and after another major snowfall, we grew tired of it. We were tired of the daily shoveling and having to be stuck inside most of the day. We started to miss our days in Hawaii with the crystal blue water and the sunny, warm days. We were all ready for it to melt.

My husband was a drill instructor on the base training the new recruits, which meant there would be long hours and some days he would have to stay overnight with them. Since his hours were so long and unpredictable, I found a job at a bank close to home with set hours to be available for our sons. Our sons were getting older. Our oldest was in high school, and a star on the basketball team. Our middle son was in junior high school and becoming popular with the girls and our youngest son was in elementary school and was very interested in writing and literature. Most of my time was spent going to basketball games and attending other school functions. My husband would attend when he could, but with his crazy work hours, most of the time, it was just me and my sons.

We lived in base housing for about a year, before we decided to buy a home. The winters in Illinois were cold, miserable, and long. So cold that we had a heater in the garage to keep our cars warm. Once we were settled in our home, and the weather got warmer, my husband bought a boat. So as soon as the weather started to warm up, we took advantage of it. Every chance we got, we were out on the lake. We lived by the Chain O'Lakes which is a waterway composed of 15 lakes connected by the Fox River and man-made channels. While my husband fished, I'd lay back, soak in the sun and read a book. On the days we took our sons, we went tubing and had water gun fights with other people who were out on the lake. I looked forward to those days, so much that I planned my work schedule to make sure I was off when my husband was off. I didn't want to miss out.

The fights and the arguments between my husband and I became less and less. I felt as though we were finally becoming one. There were nights where we'd lay in bed talking and laughing all night, just like we used to when we were first married. There were mornings where he woke me up by kissing me on the back of my neck, while he whispered sexy things in my ear. I was falling in love all over again with my husband, and I loved the way he made me feel. I started to envision the fairy tale life that I dreamed about.

My husband never stopped drinking, I just started to drink with him. I figured if he was at home drinking with me and not out drinking with his friends, I could control how much he drank. I wasn't much of a drinker, but I'd sometimes have a glass of wine with him. Some nights, we sat out on the back porch and talked about life. On one of those evenings, while sitting on the back porch, my husband started asking me about my thoughts and my opinions on our marriage. This caught me off guard because it was something he hadn't done in a while. At first I was a little scared to say anything. I didn't want to provoke him or start an argument. He sensed my hesitation, and he asked me again, saying he genuinely wanted to know my thoughts. I began to share. I shared that I loved him, but I felt as though he didn't respect me as his wife or partner. In those moments sitting there talking with him, I felt heard. He didn't interrupt me once, and he looked me in the eye. I went to bed that night feeling at peace with our marriage.

Fridays were busy days in our house. Most Fridays, my oldest son had basketball games, my middle son had guitar lessons and my youngest son was my hanging partner. With three sons, there was always somewhere to go and something that needed to be done. Since my older son was at the age where he could drive, we bought him a used car to help out.

One particular Friday evening, I was on my way out the door to take my middle son to his guitar lesson. My oldest son asked if it was okay for him to go and meet up with some friends from school. As I rushed out the door, I said yes. Later that evening, after arriving back at the house, I was sitting in the kitchen talking with two of our sons when my husband walked in. He asked where our oldest son was, and I told him that he went to meet up with some friends. My husband became upset. I asked him why he was so upset. He said that our son wasn't allowed to use his car without his permission. I knew we had grounded him earlier that month for not coming home on time, but I had made a judgement call. I didn't see any harm in letting him use the car. Earlier that week, my husband had allowed him to drive the car to the store to pick up something for him.

Right there in the kitchen, in front of our sons my husband got up in my face and told me it wasn't my judgement call to make and that I shouldn't undermine his authority. I explained to him that I wasn't undermining him. He interrupted me and yelled that he was the head of the house and not me. Again, I explained that I understood he was the head of the house, and I didn't see the harm in letting our son use the car. Once I said that, he slapped me right in front of our sons. I instantly raised my hands and covered up my face. Then he hit me again, turned and left the room.

I stood there in shock, with my head down. My two youngest sons had seen the whole thing. I felt embarrassed and ashamed. My lips started to quiver and I could feel my eyes becoming filled with tears. But I wasn't going to cry in front of our sons. In my mind, if they saw me cry, it would show weakness. I looked at them as they stood there looking at me, and I could see in their eyes how shocked and helpless they felt. I told them I was okay and to go and watch T.V. in the den.

I left the kitchen and went into the bathroom. Once I was in the bathroom, I checked to see if where he hit me was bruised. Standing there looking in the mirror made the tears start flowing. I got undressed and got in the shower to cry alone. I stood there in shower thinking about how stupid I had been to think things were better between us. It was dumb of me to think things were different.

I stayed in the bathroom for hours. I didn't want to come out until everyone was asleep. I couldn't face my sons. When I thought everyone was asleep, I came out of the bathroom, grabbed a blanket and cried myself to sleep on the couch. My husband must have left while I was in the bathroom, because later that night I heard him come in. I heard him go into our bedroom and shut the door. He never said a word. That Saturday morning, I heard my husband leave the house. Shortly after that our middle son came into the room where I was laying and gave me a hug. I couldn't even look him in the eyes. I thought about what kind of example I was setting for my sons by staying in an abusive marriage.

I stayed in the house all day feeling sorry for myself, feeling defeated and feeling stupid. My husband came home later that day and we stayed out of each other's way. I kept waiting for an apology, but I knew I would never get one. Neither one of us ever said anything about what happened the night before, and I never challenged his rules again. After that day, I became guarded once again, and I felt that little spark of peace I was feeling fade away. The suicidal thoughts I thought I had buried deep inside of me began to surface, and I started drinking more to calm them. I began to eat to fill the emptiness and the loneliness I felt. For the first time, I had come to the realization that this was my reality and it was filled with verbal, emotional, and physical abuse. My husband didn't respect me, and I was too afraid to demand it. He treated me like a piece of property that he shined up on when he was in front of his friends and tarnished and torn down in private.

After that fight, our marriage went back into the cycle of confusion I was used to. I started dreading the weekends again. The weekends were no longer days where we spent hours on the lake or sitting on the back porch talking and laughing. The weekends became days where my husband spent time with his friends drinking. I started to notice that on Friday mornings this nauseating feeling would come over me and the whole day I'd feel sick. I felt this because I wouldn't know what to expect when he came home. Some nights, he came home and went straight to bed. On those nights, I could feel all the tension I had been carrying all day from not knowing what to expect to exhale from my body. But on other nights, when "Butch" showed up, I knew it would be a long night because he'd be looking for a fight. He'd have this look about him; a look I knew all too well. His eyes were dark and cold, and every word that came out of his mouth was mean and hateful.

The nights when "Butch" showed up, he'd be in full force. As soon as he came in from being out with his friends, he wasted no time degrading me. The way I looked was always a main topic. I'll admit, I had gained some weight. Food had become a source of comfort for me. Because of the long winters, I was no longer going on my runs. I had recently cut off all my hair and started the process of growing locs, but I was still maintaining my appearance. Hell, other men still found me attractive. Why didn't he? Next he criticized our sex life, letting me know how bored he was. Once he was done depleting me of my dignity, he'd let me know that I was nothing without him. These rants would go on for hours, with me defending myself into exhaustion. I'd literally lose my voice. Once I could no longer talk, I'd just sit there emotionless, staring into space, waiting for him to grow tired of listening to himself or until he passed out.

One Friday evening while "Butch" was making an appearance, he told me he was no longer happy with me, and he was leaving. As I sat there and listening to everything he said, I thought about how stupid I had been. I had been married to this man for 14 years and most of those years I had been constantly changing myself, trying to meet his standards and trying to make him happy, while I was miserable. What about my happiness? Now here he was telling me that all I had done wasn't enough. As he continued to talk, I came to the realization that this dream I had in my mind about my marriage was just that... a dream. Once he finished, he went into the room and went to bed. I sat there in the den on the couch, feeling numb and lifeless. For some odd reason, I wasn't upset. I knew I had done everything he had asked of me, and I was relieved that he finally admitted that he wasn't in love with me anymore. But the other side of me thought, "what's so wrong with me?" I had been a good wife to him. I stayed in the den that night and I tried to cry, but I was so emotionally drained that I couldn't. Eventually I fell asleep. The next morning, we both got up and didn't say a word to each other. He left and I left with our sons. When I came home from being out my husband had moved out. I wasn't even angry or upset that he was gone. I cooked dinner for our sons and we ate.

After dinner we watched T.V. together laughing and talking and then we all got ready for bed. The house was peaceful, and I fell right to sleep. I didn't even miss him.

Two weeks went by and things around the house were normal. No one talked about my husband not being there; I think we were all enjoying the calmness. But by the third week I found myself lying in bed asking myself over and over if it was my fault he left and wondering what had I done wrong and why I wasn't enough for him. Why didn't he love me? Then I worried about how I was going to make it. I had a job, but he was and had always been the main provider. There was no way I could maintain the lifestyle our sons and I were used to. How was I going to tell my family? What would they think once they found out? Would they see me as a failure? I thought about our sons; would they blame me because he left? With all of these thoughts, fears and insecurities running through my head, I concluded that I needed to restore my marriage. I needed to convince my husband to come back home. My marriage could not fail, my self-esteem could not handle the judgement of others if it did.

I started calling him on his cell phone. I finally wanted to talk. We had not talked since he left. I wanted him to come back home and I wanted to work things out. I wanted him to tell me what I had done wrong. I wanted to know what I needed to do to make things right. I was willing to do whatever it took. This was my reality. I could not see myself or my life without him. After much talking and pleading with my husband, he came back home. I was glad he was home, but the way I felt about him was different. I still loved him, but I wasn't in love with him, and I wondered if I'd ever be in love with him again. I was getting older and I was becoming tired of his constant demands and his unattainable standards. I was tired of his temper tantrums and the drinking.

I was shocked when he agreed to come back and a part of me wondered why. If he meant all of those things he told me, and if he could do better, why was he settling for me. Even though I wondered about all of these things, I felt as though I couldn't let go of him or our marriage. A part of me felt deserving of the way he treated me. In my warped view of myself, I was unable to see myself as deserving of better.

As usual, we never talked about why he left. We never talked about the abuse. We never had a conversation on what needed to be done to repair our relationship. We just continued on like it never happened, which left me to guess or try to figure out how I was to make him happy. Me trying to figure how to become this imaginary woman my husband had in his head. I had already given so much in this marriage, but I was willing to give more because I wanted his approval desperately and I yearned to be loved.

CHAPTER 6

RECKLESS LOVE

"If it's destroying you, then it isn't love, my dear."

– UNKNOWN

In 2003, my husband received military orders to be a Naval Recruiter in Beaumont, Texas, which is only 4 hours away from Dallas. As always, moving to a new city was a new beginning. A chance to get it right. My oldest son graduated from high school before we left Illinois and enlisted in the Air Force. My middle son was in high school and my youngest was about to start middle school. They really weren't too excited about the move, but they knew that moving was a part of being a military family. I had mixed feelings about moving back to Texas. A part of me was happy to be close to family, and a part of me was uneasy. I left Texas at 18. I had run away from my past, the ridicule of others and my failures. Failures my husband always made sure I would not forget, by reminding me of them every chance he got and making it hard for me to heal the brokenness inside of me.

We found and bought a house that was big enough for the four of us and our three dogs. Our new home even had a pool in the backyard. The house needed a lot of work, so we spent the first couple of months remodeling. Every day we'd get up and go to Home Depot or Lowe's buying everything we needed to update the house. Our days were spent painting, changing out light fixtures and doing yard work. In the evening, everyone would change into their swim clothes and go for a swim. My husband would fire up the grill while I cooked some sides. The rest of the evening was spent eating and enjoying the pool. To relax, my husband would drink beer and sometimes I'd pour myself a glass of wine. Then we all passed out from exhaustion, wake up the next morning and do it all over again.

Even though I struggled with my love for my husband, I was determined to prove I could be the perfect wife. I wanted him to know that I could reach his standards, and even surpass them. In public and around our sons, I made sure to portray the image that we were on one accord.

As a young girl living in my mother's house, I had learned how to keep my feelings deep inside, so I had no problem pretending. Throughout the years of my marriage I had learned to never question or challenge my husband. So here I was this groomed up doll-wife with a painted-on smile. All I wanted to do was to keep the peace in our home. I never knew why he left when we lived in Illinois, and even though I told myself to let it go, I couldn't. I wanted so badly to get an explanation from him, but I was too afraid to demand it.

I despised him for allowing me to feel this way. I could feel those feelings of resentment each time he touched me, which made it hard for me to be intimate or affectionate with him. I couldn't understand why he wanted to be intimate with me. After all, he told me more than once that sex with me had become boring and routine. He told me numerous times he was tired of having the "same old pussy." He constantly compared me to other women, calling me fat, which made me feel inadequate. So, if I was all those things, why did he come back? Why does he stay? These questions continuously ran through my mind.

On top of repressing my feelings of bitterness and inadequacies, I was having no success finding a job. I knew it would only be a matter of time before the arguments over money would start. After months of looking, my husband suggested that maybe I should get my real estate license. We owned a few rental properties, and I handled the management side of it, such as collecting rent, making maintenance calls, and showing vacant units. I never thought about being a Realtor, but it sounded like an excellent idea. I'd be my own boss and I'd be able to work my own hours, which meant I'd be home.

After some research, I found a school that offered evening and weekend classes, so I signed up. On the first day of class, I was so nervous. Once I saw we were required to learn the principles of real estate, contract law and real estate finance; I felt overwhelmed. I was a highschool dropout. Would I be able to learn all of this? My instructor saw the panic on my face and assured me that as long as I studied and came to class, everything would eventually make sense. I said okay. But as I looked around the classroom at the other students, who looked more knowledgeable and more educated than me, it was hard to calm the nervous energy surging through my body. It took about a week for me to get past this anxious feeling, but soon I found myself looking forward to going to class. I was learning so much and the daily interactions helped my self- esteem. I could see myself being a phenomenal Realtor and building a successful business. Things at home were normal, what I considered our normal, which was me doing whatever it took to keep the peace. I didn't want "Butch" to show up.

The day I took my real estate test, I woke up feeling anxious, scared, and confident all at the same time. I was confident that I studied everything I needed to know, but I felt butterflies on the inside because I did not know what to expect. Our instructor had told the class it was a timed test with multiple choice and essay questions. Upon my arrival at the test site, I sat in my car debating if I should go in. Once I entered the room, I saw there were about twenty desks with computers at each desk. Some other people were already there to take the test, so I quickly found a desk and sat down. We sat for what felt like forever before the proctor came in to explain to us how to log in and told us to begin. Once I completed the test, I waited at my seat for the proctor to check my answers. Sitting there waiting, I could feel all the fluttering sensations going crazy inside of me again. It was so intense that I couldn't sit still. We were not allowed to bring anything into the room, so all I could do was sit there and wait. I kept looking around the room at all the people still taking the test. I glanced back at the front of the room to see if the proctor was done grading my test. After a few minutes, I was called up to his desk and with a big smile on his face, he told me I passed. When I heard him say that, a huge smile came over my face and I laughed loudly. I couldn't believe I passed the first time!

Everyone at the testing site congratulated me. Not too many people pass on their first try. I called home to let everyone know I passed and the whole drive home, I could not stop smiling. I couldn't believe I had passed. When I got home, my sons greeted me at the door with hugs and a card telling me how proud they were of me. I was really excited and I thought my husband would be excited too, since it was his idea, but there was nothing. I was expecting a special dinner or a celebration party, but there was nothing. His reaction made me wonder if he was shocked that I passed. Maybe he was waiting for me to fail because that is how he saw me: as a failure.

While waiting for my license to arrive in the mail, I started looking for a broker to sponsor me. Once I found someone, I got busy building my real estate business. I had something to prove to my husband and to myself. I was not a failure. I was determined to be successful. Soon, my ambition started causing problems in my marriage. First, we argued over money. A lot of money was going out to help build my business, but nothing was coming in. Once I started bringing in income, we argued because I was working a lot of hours, therefore never at home. Yes, I was working a lot, but I was building a business. I needed to network and meet people. He constantly wanted to know where I was and who I was meeting. He'd show up at my open houses, and I found out later from my broker that he had been calling my clients. Even though I was dealing with my husband's disruptive behavior, my hard work was starting to pay off. In my first year as a Realtor, I was considered a top producer with over a million dollars in sales. My clientele list was rapidly growing, and a lot of my past clients were referring me to new clients. My name was getting out there and other Realtors were taking notice. The more my business progressed, the more we argued. I wasn't home enough. I was neglecting the family. I wasn't being a dutiful wife. I felt as though he saw my success as a threat. I tried to explain to him that I was building a business and everything I was doing was for us and our family, but he didn't see it that way.

One evening after I came in from work, we were sitting in the kitchen talking, and I looked over at him and I saw someone familiar. I had not seen this person in a long time. I was no longer talking to my husband; I was having a conversation with "Butch". I could hear the contentment in his voice. His hazel eyes were now black and filled with rage. I got up to leave the kitchen and go into our bedroom. He got up and followed me. Before I could reach the hallway to our bedroom, I heard my husband call me a tramp. He then accused me of having an affair with a female client. I had sold this woman a home, and we had become friends through the process. I'd introduced him to her, and she had been to our house more than once. She had a son in the Air Force, just like I did.

I laughed at first because I am not gay. When he kept saying it, I realized he was serious, and I knew "Butch" was looking for a fight. He told me that he had looked at the phone records and we talked to each other too much when he wasn't around. He didn't like that I was having a relationship outside of ours. He asked me over and over what we talked about. I sat there, bewildered. I could not believe this was happening. I kept saying to him I am not gay, but he kept insisting I was. I became annoyed, irritated and afraid. I was not having an affair with this woman. Then "Butch" told me he had called her and confronted her about the relationship.

At that moment, I was pissed and disheartened. Something inside of me wondered why I continued to stay in this marriage. I lost all confidence in my husband. I felt demoralized. What was so wrong with me having a friendship with another woman? What was so wrong with me having relationships outside of ours? I was his wife and he was treating me like a child. I didn't even know how to respond. I just sat on the bed staring into space while he continued with the verbal abuse. "Butch" called me a slut and told me I was nothing but trash. I never looked at him. I was hoping he would just leave the room. Then he charged at me and started punching me all over my body. All I could do was crawl into a ball and cover up to protect myself.

My son, who was about 16 years old, heard us fighting and came out of his room and pulled my husband off of me, but he kept charging at me. I was so afraid that I ran and called the police. I told the police that someone was attacking me and I needed help. When my husband heard me on the phone with the police, he left the house. Within minutes the police were knocking on our door. I opened the door, and not wanting my husband to get arrested, I lied and said that I thought someone was in our backyard. They checked the yard and then they left. After they left, I packed some clothes and went and stayed in a hotel that night. I didn't want to be there when he came back.

On my way to the hotel, I held back tears as I checked myself in the mirror to make sure there were no bruises showing. Once I checked in and made it to my room, I closed the door, fell on the bed, and started to cry uncontrollably. I was so ashamed that my son had to come and protect me. This was not the first time he had seen his dad hit me, but it was the first time he had to stop him. I yelled, "screw him," into the air.

I told myself I was going to leave him. I wanted out of this marriage. I vented my frustration to myself for about an hour. I was so upset with myself for not having him arrested. Mad at myself for always protecting him when he didn't give a damn about hurting me. After an hour, I finally calmed myself down. Laying on the hotel bed, I wondered what had I done to make him accuse me of having an affair. Even though I had told myself I was leaving, I already knew I wasn't going anywhere. Deep down inside, I knew I would forgive him and go back. I didn't have the courage or the confidence to leave. Why couldn't I see I deserved better? I stayed at the hotel for a couple of days, ignoring the phone calls from my husband, and since I worked for myself, I didn't have to go into any office. Finally, I answered my cell phone and I could hear my husband's voice asking me when I was coming home. I wanted to say never, but I told him tomorrow and then I hung up. One more day of peace, I said to myself. To be honest, I really didn't know when I was or if I was ever going home. I was confused about what I wanted to do. I felt as though I had nowhere to go. If I left, people would wonder why and I would have to explain all that I had endured. No longer could I hide behind the persona I had created. Everyone would know my secret. I stayed one more day and then I went home. It was the only life I knew. It was my reality.

Once I was back at home, my husband showed no remorse for anything he had done. Instead, he blamed me for everything. He made the comment that I knew he was jealous hearted. This left me perplexed. How was it my fault? Was I not allowed to have friends? I felt as though he did all of this intentionally. He knew I'd end the friendship, because I'd be too embarrassed to continue the friendship. He knew I'd end it to keep the peace at home. He was right. I never talked to her after that. But one day while out shopping, I ran into her. We said hello to each other and before I could walk away, she shared with me that she was once in a relationship just like mine. It was controlling and abusive. She told me it took a lot for her to leave it, but she did. She went on to say that I was in denial about my marriage. She explained that I needed to accept that my husband's behavior was narcissistic. She told me she missed our friendship, but until I was ready to accept my circumstances and seek help, she could not be friends with me. I understood because I knew there were issues in my marriage, and she was correct about me not being ready to accept them.

A few months later, I found out my husband was having an affair again. This was the second affair that I knew of. The first one was in Corpus Christi, and over the years I always felt there were more, especially when we lived in Illinois, but I choose to ignore my feelings. I found this out because he got drunk one night and bragged about it to me. He had this proud look on his face, and he started taunting me with the facts of the affair. The woman had even been to our home. He told me how they met at hotels, and the things they did.

A part of me really didn't care that he was having an affair. I didn't miss having sex with him. I had lost those feelings a long time ago. I did become infuriated because here he was accusing me of being gay and sleeping with a woman, when all along it was him having the affairs. In my anger, I called him a drunk and a loser. I told him I couldn't believe I had wasted most of my life loving him. In an egotistical way, he told me it was my fault he kept having affairs. If I was a better wife, if I took better care of myself, if I were more intimate with him, he would not have the desire to have an affair. He laughed while telling me I was replaceable and how women came on to him all the time.

While I listened to him go on with his rant, I thought about our time in Illinois. I should have never begged him to come back. I should have divorced him then. While he continued with his bragging about all the women he could have, I calmly walked into our bedroom, grabbed some clothes and I left the house. I wasn't going to stay there and subject myself to his belittlement. I drove to a hotel and I got a room for the night. I just wanted to be alone. I just wanted some peace.

The first thing I did when I got to my room was to turn off my cell phone. I fell into the bed and I didn't cry. I just blamed myself for staying in the loveless marriage for so long. I didn't know why I stayed. Deep down, a part of me believed I deserved to be treated this way. Most of my life, all I ever heard from the people who supposedly loved me was how I was useless, a liar, and I wouldn't amount to anything. I believed every word of it. When people say or do things that align with what you are already thinking and feeling about yourself, it's hard for you to believe you deserve better. That morning when I woke up, I didn't know where else to go or who to talk to, so I got dressed and drove home to my reckless life. When I arrived, my husband wasn't shocked to see me; he knew I would be back. I'd always come back. We never talked about what happened the night before. We never talked about the affair; it was like it never happened. But even though we never talked about it, something had shifted in me.

I no longer cared what my husband did. I didn't care if he was still seeing her. I wanted him to leave. I loathed lying next to him in bed each night. I detest the way he smelled. The sound of his voice made my skin crawl. I'd sleep in sweatpants and a sweatshirt because I didn't want him to touch me and the last thing I wanted to do was be intimate with him. When he'd come home from work, I'd leave the room.

Our home was filled with silence. Everything I was feeling flowed out onto the pages of my journal. I had no conversations with him anymore. I became very bitter, and you could feel the tension in the house. I tried to pretend things were okay in front of our sons, but I could sense that they knew I was unhappy. In May of that year, our middle son graduated from high school and joined the Navy. Our sons were becoming men. Our oldest son was now married and living in Florida. Our youngest son would be starting high school that following year. I often wondered what my life would be like once they were all gone. They had always been that constant comfort that I needed. When I was sad, they always knew how to cheer me up. When I felt unsure, they were always there to build me up. At times, I wondered if they knew that I needed them way more than they needed me.

Later that year, my husband told me he was taking orders to a ship in Virginia, and I was glad he was leaving. A day before he was to leave, my husband gave me divorce papers and left the house. A part of me felt relieved. But that night in bed I found myself crying.

The next day I got up and went to work and that night I laid in bed and cried. I cried because I so deeply wanted my marriage, or maybe I just wanted the fairy tale. I cried because once again I had failed. Maybe everyone was right about me; I was worthless. I cried because I couldn't understand why he didn't love me. When I was all cried out, I got mad. I wanted to hurt him, and I decided I wanted to hurt the woman he was having an affair with. I knew her name because my husband told me. So, I started trying to figure out where she lived and where she worked. I wanted to confront her. Someone was going to feel my pain. I was the person who had endured verbal and physical abuse, not her. Didn't that count for something? Now he wanted a divorce so he could be with her. I took those divorce papers and I shredded them. I called and told my husband I wasn't signing any damn papers. You don't get to come in and destroy my life and leave, I told him. Then I hung up the phone and cried.

Early one morning, I was awakened by the phone ringing. Thinking it was my husband, I grabbed the phone and found my cousin from Kansas City on the phone. She was calling to let me know that my uncle had died. I started crying hysterically. I didn't know my dad. In my eyes, my uncle had been the father figure in my life. I had learned so much from him. He taught me so much about life and how to love unconditionally. I knew he had been sick and normally I'd called every week to check on him, but in the last month I had been so preoccupied with my marriage that the calls became less and less. Mainly because I didn't want my aunt and uncle to know what I was going through.

As I sat on the edge of my bed and wiped the tears from my eyes, I felt so guilty for not calling more, for not visiting more. I thought about my aunt; my uncle was the love of her life. I knew she was heartbroken. My cousin gave me all the details of when the funeral was going to be. We said our goodbyes and hung up. I fell back into bed and cried some more. After I calmed down, I worked up the courage and called my husband. I really don't know why I called him. We hadn't spoken to each other in over a month. I was hurting, and I just wanted to be consoled. When he answered, I could instantly tell by the tone of his voice that he didn't want to talk to me. He made me feel as though I was bothering or interrupting him. I told him about my uncle's death, and I asked if he could come home and go with me to the funeral. When I finished, there was silence. He told me he was sorry to hear about my uncle and because of work, he would not be able to attend the service. I said okay and hung up. I knew that was bullshit. He could come home if he wanted to. Then I became upset with myself for calling him. Why did I expect him to care that I was hurting?

On the flight back from Kansas City, I had a lot of time to reminisce about my childhood. Being back at 3609 College had stirred up a lot of memories. I thought about the love I felt in that house as a child and how I yearned for that same love once I left. I wanted a relationship like my aunt and uncle. I wanted the fairy tale. I wanted to experience a breathtaking love. I deserved it. On that flight, I decided I was going to show my husband he made a mistake filing for a divorce. I wanted him to know that he could never replace me. Once I returned from the funeral, I started running again, to lose weight and to take my mind off of things. Each day at 4:30 am I'd get up, put on my workout clothes, place my shoulder length locs in a ponytail, head to the gym and run three miles on the treadmill. Then I would meet up with a workout group for some strength training. I started reading again. Mainly to build my self-respect and my self-esteem. If I wanted respect from my husband, I needed to be confident about who I was. Over the next month, I made it a point to show myself love. I started getting facials, manicures and pedicures. I meditated in the mornings and every day, including Saturday, I got dressed, did my hair and my makeup. I told myself I'll fix myself and once my husband sees the person I was becoming, he would want to come back. I was going to show him how wrong he was about me.

I was on this fixation to prove my husband wrong, because deep down inside, I missed him. After all the things he had put me through,

I couldn't see myself living without him. I desperately wanted my marriage to work. I didn't want it to fail. A few months before his tour was over in Virginia, I reached out to my husband. We talked about everything I had been doing, and I asked him if he still wanted the divorce. He told me he was unsure. I asked if he wanted to try to work things out. His reply was he needed to think about it. So, I gave him space. Soon, our telephone calls became more frequent. Phone calls turned into text messages. Then those text messages turned into emails. Emails turned into longer telephone calls where we really talked.

In one of those conversations, we agreed to put the past behind us and we both agreed to stop the divorce. I expressed how I needed to be treated differently, with respect, and he said he understood. It was like we were dating and getting to know each other all over again. I looked forward to our conversations each day. When his tour in Virginia was over, I flew up to Virginia and helped him move back to Beaumont to our house. We drove back, stopping along the way to visit family and friends. It was like we were on our honeymoon. We walked around holding hands like we were newlyweds. I thought, maybe there is a chance for us. Maybe there is a chance for us to live in peace.

CHAPTER 7

DEJAVU

> "A person doesn't have to hit you for it to be abuse. They can degrade, humiliate, blame, curse, manipulate or try to control you; it's all abuse."
>
> –Unknown

Even though we were not moving to a new city, I considered my husband coming back home to a new beginning. Once back in Beaumont, my husband retired from the military. He quickly found employment working as a sales representative for a beverage company. This job came with set hours, no weekends, and a company vehicle. I felt it was best for our marriage for me to leave the pressures of being a Realtor. My business had grown a lot, and I was successful at it, but I felt as though my home life was more important. I thought about all the arguments we had about my business before he left, so I decided to find a job that would be less stressful. I soon found employment working at a bank. The hours were stable and I was home most weekends. Our home life was calm and I looked forward to coming home every day. We ate dinner together. We would meet up for lunch and there was the weekly date night. At night we laid in bed talking and laughing with each other. Our conversations were playful and intimate.

Our youngest son was graduating from high school in May of that year and soon my husband and I would be empty nesters. My sons were a consistent and effortless source of happiness in my life. Being around them relaxed me. The thought of all our sons being gone stirred up a lot of emotions inside of me. I tried to picture what life would be like with just my husband and I. Things had been going well, and I felt as though we were finally living as one. I didn't want this peace I felt to end. One evening while eating dinner, my husband told me about a job opportunity with his company in Dallas. After some discussion, we decided he should apply for the job. A couple of weeks later, he drove up to Dallas and stayed with family so he could interview.

Within days, we found out that he got the job. We were on the move again. This time moving back to our hometown. I had mixed feelings about the move. A part of me was thrilled and thought this was an excellent way to start the second half of our life. We had spent most of our youth moving from duty station to duty station, only coming home to visit maybe once a year. A part of me was apprehensive about the move. I was going back to the place I so desperately wanted to leave so many years ago. The more I thought about the move, I felt it was a good thing. We would be living closer to our family and we could reconnect. I told myself this was my chance to heal and to repair the relationship with my mother. Though we were cordial to each other, I still held some harsh feelings and animosity towards her for past hurts.

When I first left Texas, there was little to no communication between the two of us. When we did communicate, it was over the telephone, and we mostly talked about my sons. When I did come to Dallas to visit, we always stayed at my mother-in-law's house and I'd drop my sons off at my mother's house to visit. She hardly ever came to visit us, and when she did, I'd feel uneasy waiting for her to ridicule me about my parenting skills. But now that I was older and moving back to Dallas, I wanted to try to build more than a cordial relationship with her. After some deep prayers and some conversations with my aunt in Kansas City, I decided it was time to let go of the past and move forward.

In April 2009 we put our home in Beaumont on the market and started looking for a home in Dallas. My husband moved to Dallas and stayed with family, and I would move there once our youngest son graduated in May. We found a home in Dallas that we both fell in love with at first sight. It sat on an acre lot with a large circle driveway. It needed a lot of work, but we could handle it. I loved the whole idea that it needed work. I loved the thought of picking out paint colors, flooring and kitchen appliances. I couldn't wait to get started. After my son's graduation, we loaded up the U-Haul with all our possessions and made the four-hour drive to Dallas. My youngest son stayed with us for about a month before enlisting in the Air Force. Once we were all moved in, we started to get reacquainted with family members and friends we had not seen in a long time. We held a big barbeque and invited everyone over. It was like a family reunion. People I had not seen for over 20 years were there. The house was filled with laughter and we all spent the day catching up with each other's lives.

Dallas had changed a lot over the years. A lot of the places we remembered were no longer there and there was construction everywhere. I spent a lot of time getting lost and trying to find my way around. Every day was an adventure, and I enjoyed every minute of it. One weekend, my sister called and asked if I wanted to go with her and my cousin to have a girl's day checking out contemporary furniture and antique stores in the Design District. I had never been to the Design District, and I looked forward to going and getting ideas for our new home. I was also looking forward to hanging out with my sister. We spent most of the day going from store to store, looking at all kinds of art and furniture. My mind was filled with so many ideas and I couldn't wait to get back and share them with my husband. On the way home, my sister took me to see more of my family who I had not seen in years. We were all glad to see each other and, after spending a couple of hours getting reacquainted, we all exchanged numbers. When I arrived home, I shared with my husband about all the cool stuff I saw in the Design District and all the ideas I had for our home. I also shared how excited I was that I got to see more family that I had not seen in years. It was a good day.

The more I spent time with my family, the more I realized that I had missed so much. Cousins that were small kids when I left were now young adults with their own kids that I didn't even know.

One evening while my husband and I were watching T.V. my cell phone rang. It was one of my cousins I had seen when I was out with my sister. We talked on the phone for a few minutes, and I invited him over so we could catch up more. We said our goodbyes and I hung up. My husband asked who I was talking to, and I told him it was my cousin. He asked why he was calling me and I explained that we exchanged numbers so we could keep in touch. My husband then stood up from his chair and made it clear that no man should be calling me. He said he didn't care if it was family or not. I became irritated with his response. This was my cousin, not some stranger off the street. Besides, I was a grown woman, not some child he could place stipulations on. I instantly saw what was going on. It was deja vu. I had seen it in Hawaii, Illinois and in Beaumont. This was his way of keeping control over our relationship. This was him finding a way to play on my emotions rather than using logic and reasoning.

He'd already expressed that I was spending too much time visiting with my family and now he was looking for a way to cause division. But this time, instead of being a coward, I took a stance. I wanted to be able to see my family, all of them: male or female. So, we argued about this for days. There was a lot of tension in the house, but I didn't care. Each time he attempted to pressure me to go along with his way of thinking by suggesting that all people thought the way he did, I let him know I didn't care; I was not changing the way I felt. I was going to see my family.

After a few days of silence in the house, he realized that I was not going to yield, and he made what I thought was peace. He agreed that maybe he was being too controlling. At that moment, I felt victorious. For the first time in our marriage, I had stood my ground.

That October, for my aunt's birthday, some of us decided to get together and take her to lunch. Me, my aunt and my mother all loaded up in my sister's car, while everyone else loaded up in another car, and we all went to Pappadeauxs, a seafood restaurant. On the way there, we laughed, cracked jokes and enjoyed each other's company. While we were waiting on our table, my nephew called my sister, and he decided he wanted to join us. After my nephew arrived, we were shown to our table, where the laughter continued. We talked about men, relationships, and other women. No topic was off limits, and a few times my nephew had to cover his ears. While we were waiting for our food, I noticed how much my mother had changed. Her hair was fixed, she had on makeup, and she seemed at peace with herself. This encouraged me even more to fix our relationship. I wanted to know this woman, so I could erase the woman that I remembered from my childhood.

Before our food arrived, we all crowded around my aunt and took a group picture to post on her Facebook page. When our food arrived, we all started to eat. We all sampled food from each other's plates, sharing what we liked and what we didn't like. It was a good day and we all were having a good time. While we ate, I received a call from my husband. When I answered, he told me he could not find one of our dogs. He told me he had looked all over the house, but the dog was nowhere in sight. I could tell he was drinking because he was slurring his words. He wanted me to come home right away. I knew I couldn't leave. We all rode together in my sister's car, and I wasn't about to ask everyone to hurry and eat just so I could leave. I explained this to him, and I assured him that if he didn't let the dog outside, then everything was okay. The dog was probably somewhere asleep. Then I hung up my cell. But he called again. He wanted me to come home.

Again, I explained that I didn't drive and it was impossible for me to leave. Everyone at the table started to see how frustrated and annoyed I was becoming. In my mind, I knew there was nothing wrong with the dog. My husband was just drunk. After the third call, my nephew offered to leave and go over to my house to make sure everything was okay. I was reluctant to let my nephew leave, but he insisted. So he left and we continued to eat. About 30 minutes later, my nephew called and told me that my dog greeted him at the door when he arrived at my house, just as I suspected.

That evening when I arrived home, my husband looked at me and told me he did not care if I was with Jesus, "when I call, you come" was his comment to me. In that moment, I knew "Butch" had arrived. I had not seen "Butch" since we had moved back to Dallas, and I didn't miss him. I could feel the rage inside of me start to rise up, but I didn't say a word. I just looked at him. Then I turned and went into the bedroom. While I walked to our bedroom, I prayed that he would not follow me. I prayed that he'd just pass out in his recliner. I sat on the bed fully dressed, because I told myself I needed to be dressed, so I could leave in a hurry if he started a fight. I sat there nervously for about an hour. Then I walked into the T.V. room and saw that he had fallen asleep. Once I knew he was sleeping, I could feel all the nervous energy leave my body, and I let out a sigh of relief. I went into our bedroom, shut the door, and got ready for bed. I didn't sleep much that night. I kept waking up and making sure he was still asleep. That morning, he came into our bedroom and asked me if I wanted any breakfast, as if nothing had happened the night before. I told him no, and we never talked about what happened the night before.

Three months after moving back to Dallas, I found a job as an accounts payable clerk for a small business that owned restaurants. It was close to home with set hours. I didn't want to work anywhere that demanded a lot of me. I just wanted to go to work and be able to come home. I didn't want to cause any problems at home. Besides, the house we bought needed a lot of attention. It had sat vacant for a very long time before we bought it. We knew all of this when we bought the house, but it had so much potential. This was going to be our final home, so we were up for the challenge. At least that is what I thought. We were making a lot of repairs to the house, and before long, arguments started over me not contributing enough to our finances. The more stress we'd encounter with the repairs of the house, the more he'd drink. And the more he'd drink, the more I became a target for his verbal attacks. He'd tell me how unappreciative I was of all the sacrifices he had made for us. That I didn't love him and how he could do better without me. Then he'd wake up the next day like nothing happened the night before. He'd want to talk about his ideas on how to rebuild the deck in the backyard, or the type of grass to plant in the front yard. It was like living with two different people. I soon started to dread coming home, especially on the weekends. I never knew who I was coming home to. Would my husband greet me at the door or would "Butch"? I'd get this queasy feeling inside each day when it got close to time for me to get off. Never knowing what to expect gave me a nervous, restless energy.

I soon noticed myself slipping back into a box of gloom. The weight I lost I had gained all back. My menstrual cycles became irregular from the stress. I stopped styling my locs, and a ponytail became my everyday look, and I didn't take the time to put on makeup anymore. Eczema patches started showing up all over my body. As our disagreements turned into fights, the suicidal thoughts once again started to invade my dreams. I felt it was my only way out of this life. Nothing in my marriage had changed; it seemed as though it was getting worse. I wanted my marriage to work, but I didn't know how to compete with a bottle or with "Butch".

In December 2009, I began planning for my sons to come home for Christmas. I was so excited. We were all going to be in the same house, and I couldn't wait. Early one morning, I was awakened by a phone ringing. It was my sister. She told me that my cousin had been trying to reach me to let me know that my aunt in Kansas City had suffered a stroke. My whole body went numb, I don't even remember anything else that was said from the conversation with my sister. I just started crying. My husband asked me what was going on, and I told him my aunt had a stroke. He put his arms around me to console me. It surprised me when he wrapped his arms around me and held me. He hadn't held me in a long time. As I laid in his arms, I thought about all the conversations my aunt and I had. After my uncle passed, I made it a point to call more often. I thought about all the things I was too ashamed to share, but somehow I felt as though she knew. She was so easy to talk to and always offered words of wisdom. During the calls she shared her advice, never judging, and at the end of every call she'd pray for me and let me know that I was loved. My aunt would always ask me if I had found a church yet. When I said no, her response would be "you need a church family around you". I was going to miss her.

The next morning, I started planning to go to Kansas City. My husband and I knew my sons were flying into Dallas for Christmas, so we both decided that he should stay home. Before I could arrive in Kansas City, my aunt passed away. I was heartbroken. I was not ready for her to die. My aunt was not my mother, but she had been a strong influence in my life. I looked to her for guidance. As a little girl, I emulated her, and as a woman, each time I saw her or talked to her, I craved to have her poise and strength. In my eyes, she embodied everything I felt a woman should be.

After returning from my aunt's funeral, I felt so lost. I don't remember much about the end of 2009. The remaining days were just a blur with me just going through the motions. I saw my aunt and uncle as my anchor; I looked to them to help keep me grounded. I knew they loved me unconditionally and now that they were gone, I felt as though I had no one.

February 2010 I went in for my annual exam. My doctor completed my physical and drew some blood so she could complete some lab work. A week later, I got a phone call from my doctor asking me to come back in. When I arrived at her office, she went over the results from my physical and my labs. The results showed excessive weight gain. My cholesterol was horrible and I was borderline hypertensive. She told me if I didn't make some changes soon; it was only a matter of time before she would have to put me on medication to control my symptoms. She asked me if I was under a lot of stress, and I lied and said no. I was not going to share with her my messed-up life. I promised her I would make some changes, and the next day I put on my running shoes and started running again. At first I struggled. It had been so long since I ran, but I encouraged myself each day to keep going. I started out slow walking and running and eventually I could run three to four miles without stopping. I was proud of myself. It was like taking back a little part of my life, and running soon became my escape from my husband and my home life.

One typical Monday at work, while on my lunch break, I surfed the internet out of boredom. An article popped up about a woman who was in an abusive relationship, so I clicked on the link. I started reading the article and it was like I was reading about my life. A lot of the things the woman shared were things I was or had experienced in my marriage. Her spouse was a very good provider and could be very loving at times. In public and to family and friends, they were the perfect couple. Everyone envied them. They had a nice car, home and a phat bank account. But what no one knew was that her husband was a master of disguise. He portrayed himself as the selfless, good guy in public, but at home, without any notice, things would change and her husband would become a totally different person. She went on to say it was like living with Dr. Jekyll and Mr. Hyde. He was very controlling and emasculating. He would call her out of name. He would humiliate and degrade her. He would blame her for everything that didn't go his way. He would ignore her, and he made her feel worthless. There was physical, verbal, and emotional abuse and he always wanted to have sex afterwards. She went on to say that the next day they would both get up and act like nothing had happened, with no apology. He'd simply buy her something really nice and expensive; that was his way of making up. It was like she was me. She was living my life. What an eye-opening experience. I thought I was the only one living this life. I felt as though no one would believe me if I ever told them about the things I was enduring behind closed doors.

After reading her story, I became curious to see if there were more stories like this one. It was comforting to see that I wasn't alone. I wanted to understand why women like she and I stayed in these relationships. This article stated women of abuse struggle with self-worth and we convince ourselves that we cause the abuse in our relationships. We are conditioned that what happens in the house stays in the house and this frame of thinking keeps us from seeking help. Asking for help shows a sign of weakness. As I continued to read, I came upon a part that said once we find our knight in shining armor, we endure what's necessary to portray the illusion to the world that we have arrived and that we are living the fairy tale.

I kept scrolling and found another article that mainly focused on African American Women and abuse. In this article it talked about how black women were the highest population in Christianity. It described how we felt a sense of security in God and believed that God would take care of us and change our abuser. We misinterpreted Bible verses and we believed that in order to be obedient to God; we had to endure this behavior. We felt stuck and helpless. Therefore, we don't get a divorce or leave the relationship. We simply pray. Leaving is not an option.

After reading those articles, it made me more aware that I could no longer ignore the problems in my marriage. I loved this man, but I started to wonder if he really loved me. He was an excellent provider. He provided all the material things I wanted and desired, but emotionally I was dying. If he truly loved me, why was he so abusive to me with his words and his actions? Why did he degrade and belittle me and make me feel worthless and cheap? Why did he deliberately misrepresent my thoughts and dreams? If he loved me, why did he see me as a slut and a whore? We had been married for over 20 years. I knew I wasn't perfect, but I had been totally committed to this man and to our marriage. I endured the abuse and the affairs. Reading about the women in those articles was like looking in a mirror. Just like those women, I looked for love and my self-worth in others. My whole life I had been told what I wasn't: I wasn't a good daughter, I wasn't a good mother, and I was a terrible wife. In my mind, I was a failure. My whole life was a lie. My lunch was over, but I couldn't shake what I had read. My husband was killing my spirit. A love that constantly tears you down isn't really love. On my way home that evening, I realized I really wanted to sit down and talk with my husband about what I had read. I wanted him to hear and understand what I was feeling. I wanted to explain to him how I felt about our relationship. I wanted him to know that we needed help. I wanted him to know that I was tired of the fighting. I wanted him to know that I loved him, but that I had fallen out of love with him.

Once I got home and walked into his office, I saw the beer bottle sitting on his desk. I knew better than to even bring up what I had read or how I was feeling. If I did share what I read, it would only start an argument and things had been calm between us for a while now. So instead of bringing up what I had read, I went over and kissed him on the forehead, went into the bedroom, changed my clothes, wrapped my long locs into a bun and went for a run. I ran until I became numb. Once I got back from my run, I took a shower; we ate dinner and watched T.V. Then we went to bed. I never brought up what I read that day.

CHAPTER 8

MOVIE NIGHT

*"When people show you who they are,
believe them the first time."*

—MAYA ANGELOU

Reading about those women on the internet whose stories were similar to mine had cracked open a wall I had built in my mind. In a weird way, those articles gave me a sense of relief. All this time, I really thought I was this woman who deserved to be abused. I thought I caused it all. I felt it was my fault when my husband became verbally, mentally, and physically abusive. After each argument or fight, I'd play the incident over and over in my head, trying to see what I had done that provoked my husband. I wanted to make sure I didn't do it again. I'd tell myself if I just listened, there would be no reason for him to treat me this way. I felt as though I was going insane. But those articles showed me that I was not alone; I was not going crazy. Over the next couple of months, I read everything I could find on abuse. I learned that in abusive relationships, most abuse starts out with verbal attacks. Then slowly the mental and psychological abuse begins. Finally, financial abuse enters the relationship. Most abusers only use physical abuse to maintain control, to bully.

I also read articles on alcoholism. I wanted to understand why my husband needed to drink. He always told me that drinking calmed his mind. I never understood how something that made him so irrational calmed his mind. His drinking was a problem, and I didn't know how I could help him. I wasn't trying to leave my husband. I wanted to save my marriage. I loved my husband. I totally believed we could have the fairy tale. I knew his drinking played a significant part in our problems. I felt as though he was self-medicating his inner demons with alcohol, and this was not the solution. But every article I read about abuse and even the articles I read on alcoholism stated that eventually someone leaves the relationship. In abusive relationships, the person being abused eventually leaves to save their own life. In relationships where one of the partners is an alcoholic, the alcoholic eventually runs off the sober partner. This made me think about how my story would end. Would I ever build up the courage to leave? Or would I stay and continue to die inside?

Now that we were empty nesters, we spent a lot of time at home watching movies. My husband didn't care much for going out; he didn't like being around people. I never knew when "Butch" was going to show up, so I didn't mind staying at home. So, we'd go to the Red Box down the street from our home, rent some DVD's and grab something to eat on the way home. The movie we chose on this particular night was Captain America, and I was excited to see it. I had read many reviews about it, and they were all good. I had heard the movie was action packed with a lot of fight scenes. I loved those kinds of movies. I could tell my husband had been drinking earlier that day while I was at work, so I was feeling a little guarded. I hoped that once the movie started, he'd pass out, and I could enjoy the movie in peace. Back at home, my husband put the movie in the DVD player while I placed our hamburgers and fries on plates. I brought out the food and handed his plate to him where he was sitting in his recliner. I grabbed my blanket and found my spot on the corner of the couch.

The movie started, and once I was done eating, I laid my head down on the arm of the couch to get more comfortable. About an hour into the movie, my husband started talking about something. I thought he was commenting on something about the movie, so I just kind of ignored him. Mostly because I couldn't understand him and I really just wanted him to go to sleep so I could continue enjoying the movie, but he kept talking. Finally, I raised up and looked at him so I could understand what he was saying. He started to tell me how he spent the day drinking with this guy he went to school with. He knew I didn't care much for this friend he was talking about, because every time they got together, they would get drunk together.

I laid my head back down and I tried to focus on the movie. But he kept going on and on about his day, and I wished he'd just be quiet. Then he told me that this friend saw my cousin, the same cousin my husband accused me of having an affair with over a month ago. This friend told my husband he believed that my cousin and I were hooking up and having sex behind his back. I raised back up because I could not believe we were having this discussion again. I thought we had moved past this. I instantly became irritated, so much so that my hands started to shake. I explained again to my husband that I was not having an affair with anyone, especially a family member. Even though I could feel myself becoming enraged, I tried to stay calm, because I could tell "Butch" had arrived and I just wanted to keep the peace. I did not want to provoke him. But at the same time, I was so tired of being accused of his stupid accusations. I had been faithful to my husband our entire marriage.

Before I could get another word out of my mouth, my husband quickly rose up from this chair and before I could get up from the couch, he was on top of me, punching me in my face and in my head. I raised my hands to cover myself up, because he did not let up. He just kept punching. I could smell the liquor on his breath. The whole time he was punching me, he was yelling, but I couldn't understand what he was saying. All I could think was, "what the hell is going on!". Every time I'd try to fight back, he'd restrained me with his body. Somehow I ended up on the floor and I tried to get away, but then he grabbed me by my locs and started dragging me around the house. At some point, he stopped punching me, placed his hands around my throat and started choking me. He kept yelling, but I couldn't comprehend what he was saying; I just kept trying to pull his hands away from my neck.

At that moment, I thought I was going to die and some part of me was ready. I was tired. I was tired of the chaos, the accusations, and the abuse. The suicidal side of me just wanted him to kill me. After what seemed like hours of him punching and choking me, I finally stopped defending myself, and I just gave up and laid there. He must have sensed that I had given up, because he pulled me up to my feet, dragged me to the front door and threw me out of the house. I heard him lock the door. As I stood outside, a part of me felt relieved. During the whole fight I felt as though I couldn't breathe, now outside I started to cough trying to catch my breath. Once I caught my breath, I became furious. "Why didn't he finish? Why didn't he kill me?" is what I thought. I ran around the house looking for a way back in; I wanted him to finish what he started. Then a voice in my head said, "Are you stupid, don't go back in there." I stopped looking for a way in. As I stood outside our home, I realized I was standing outside his home. Many times, he made it clear to me that his money bought this home, even though we both worked. I was at peace knowing that tonight was going to be the night he was going to kill me.

While I stood there, I thought about all the times I should have left him. I should have left the first time he hit me. I should have left when he accused me of being gay. I should have left when he accused me of sleeping with our neighbors and sleeping with his friends. I should have left when he accused me of sleeping with my sister's husband. I should have left when he told me he was more important than God. I should have left when he told me I was his property. I should have left a thousand times before, but I didn't. I had stayed because I believed him every time he told me things would be different. I had been so stupid. Why was I so desperate to be loved by this person who obviously didn't love me? Why was I so obsessed with someone who couldn't see my worth? Why couldn't I see my own worth? I thought of all the things I'd done to prove my love to this man. I had taken a lie detector test and passed, and he still insisted I was a whore. I had ended friendships. I had walked away from my family trying to please him. The tears started streaming uncontrollably down my face. I was ready to die that night, every inch of me wished he would have finished.

Once I realized he was not coming out of the house and a force inside of me was keeping me from going back in, I reached for my cell phone. But I didn't have it. I started to walk towards a neighbor's house, but I was too embarrassed to go knock on the door to ask for help. It soon became clear to me that I would have to do something I didn't want to do. I wiped the tears from my eyes, and with no shoes on my feet, I started to walk to my sister's house. She lived about a mile away from where I lived. To get to her house, I'd have to walk down a busy main street and across a main intersection. The whole way there, I thought *the whole family would know my secret.* I had become a professional at masquerading our problems. As I walked, I thought about what everyone would say once they found out. A few times, I thought about turning around and going back. This wasn't our first fight, and I knew once he sobered up, we would just continue living the lie.

But something deep inside of me asked, aren't you tired of this? You've been with this man most of your life and the abuse has only gotten worse. So, I continued to walk, thinking about everything I had endured in our marriage. The affairs, the verbal, mental, psychological, and physical abuse. I was so consumed in my thoughts; I didn't think about my bare feet on the concrete sidewalk. I thought about how I constantly had to walk on eggshells in my own home. The more I thought about all I had been through, my stride became faster, and I became angry with myself. *You are so stupid,* I told myself over and over. When I finally reached my sister's house, I hesitated for a moment, then I rang the doorbell. My sister opened the door, and I started crying all over again. I walked inside the house and told her what was going on. She took me into the living room, and I sat down on the couch and put my head in my hands. I felt so ashamed; I couldn't even look at her. Before I knew it, my sister had called another family member, a cousin, who showed up a few minutes later.

My sister and my cousin both stated that I should call the police, but I didn't want to. I couldn't bear the thought of him going to jail. I thought about our sons. What would they think? Would they be mad at me for having their dad arrested? After much persuasion from my sister and my cousin, I decided to call the police. Once the police arrived, they looked at my bruises and took pictures. I hadn't even looked at myself in the mirror, so while the officer took pictures, I wondered how I looked. I could taste blood in my mouth, so I knew that meant that my lip was busted, and I had a pounding headache from all the hits to my head. The officer asked a few questions, and he let me know that my husband was going to be arrested, even if I didn't want it. The officer also told my sister and my cousin that I needed to go to the hospital and be examined. I started to cry, but not because I was hurt. I was crying because I didn't want my husband to be arrested. In all the years I had been married, I'd never had my husband arrested. I knew if he was arrested, it would affect his military career, and I didn't want that to happen. I didn't want to tarnish his image. I didn't want anyone to know my secret.

Once the officer left, my sister gave me some shoes to wear and she and my cousin drove me to the hospital. At the hospital, I was examined and pictures were taken once again of my bruises. After the examination, a counselor came in and talked to me about being a victim of domestic violence. She asked if I wanted to go to a shelter. I said no. In my mind, shelters were for women who were victims. I didn't consider myself a victim. This was my normal. "What couple didn't fight?" I thought to myself. My self-esteem was so low from years of constantly being belittled that I couldn't see that my marriage was unhealthy. I couldn't see that I was truly a victim. Besides, I loved my husband and I wanted to maintain our family. I just wanted the violence to end.

I was finally released from the hospital after what seemed like forever. I walked out into the waiting room where my sister and my cousin were waiting. We walked out to my sister's car and we all got in. On the way back to my sister's house, we had to stop by my house so I could get some clothes, check on my dogs and lock up our home. As we pulled into the driveway, a police officer was there waiting. He informed us that my husband had been arrested and taken to jail for booking. I asked the police officer about our dogs, and he told me they had been placed in their kennels. As I walked into the house, I was reminded of everything that had happened that night. I saw the gun laying on the table and I thought to myself, was he going to use it on me? Why didn't he? Then this nightmare of a life would have been over, and I would finally have some peace. I saw strands of my locs that he pulled out all over the floor, and I wondered if my sister and my cousin saw it.

I stood there replaying the fight over and over in my head; it was so clear to me like a scene from a movie. I stood there and thought about what had I done to cause this madness. Not once did I think about leaving. He was my husband until death do us part. That was the vow I took. I knew eventually I'd come back. I always did. I went into our bedroom to get some clothes. I only packed enough clothes for about a week, because I knew after a week "Butch" would be gone, and I'd forgive.

I always forgave my husband. I walked into the utility room where we kept the dog kennels and checked on the dogs. I knew they would be okay overnight in their kennels, and I would get someone to check on them in the morning. I walked back into the T.V. room and told my sister, my cousin and the police I was ready to leave. We all walked outside, and I shut and locked the front door. Back in my sister's car, I stayed silent. My sister and cousin were talking, but I couldn't hear a word they were saying. It all sounded like a bunch of noise to me. I just sat there. I kept replaying the whole night over and over in my head.

The next day, I stayed home from work. I called in and told my supervisor I had been attacked. It was the truth; I just didn't tell her it was my husband who had done it. I sat in my sister's guest room on the bed and wondered what I was going to do. A part of me knew it was time to leave, but a part of me wanted to forgive him and work things out. I knew this relationship was killing me mentally and emotionally, but I just couldn't see myself not being with this man. I had been with him most of my life. Many times in our relationship, he told me how he needed me to protect him from himself. I really wanted to believe that I could protect him from his inner demons.

Around 7pm, right when I started to fall asleep, my phone rang. I looked at the caller ID and saw it was an unknown number. I answered and heard a computerized voice asking me if I wanted to accept a collect call from the Dallas County jail. In the background, I heard my husband say his name. I said yes and pressed 1 to accept his call. I sat there in silence.

When he started to speak, the tears started streaming down my face. I hated myself for having him arrested. I wanted to hang up, but for some reason I couldn't. I was angry at him for what he had done to me, but some part of me just wanted to hold him. I was filled with so much sorrow. I could tell he was still furious. I could hear the rage in his voice. There was no remorse in his voice at all. Not once did he apologize. All he told me was that he could not find anyone to bail him out of jail, so he called me. I told him I'd bail him out, and I hung up my phone. I got out of bed, got dressed, and asked my sister to go with me to find a bail bondsman. I could tell she was upset with me, but she never said a word. She just got dressed and came with me. Even if she had said something, I was still going to bail him out. I was full of regret for having him arrested. I felt as though it was my fault.

Once I found a bail bondsman, I signed the papers to have him bailed out. While my husband was being processed for his release, I took my sister back to her house. I then drove to the jail and waited for him to be released. About 45 minutes later my husband came walking out of the precinct. As he walked toward the car, a nervous feeling came over me because I didn't know what to expect. When he got in the car, I didn't even look at him, but the smell of old liquor filled the car like cheap cologne. The smell was so strong that it made me sneeze. I started the car and drove to our home. It was a silent ride. I had nothing to say to my husband. I kept waiting for the apology, even though I knew I would never get it. He never apologized or showed any remorse for his abuse. He'd always found a way to make the abuse my fault. Once we arrived at our home, we both got out of the car, and I opened the front door. I turned around to leave, and he walked over to me. I stepped back, not knowing what he was going to do. He pulled me close and whispered in my ear he didn't really remember much about the night before because he had been drinking all that day with his friend. He told me if I had just obeyed him, he wouldn't have to hit me. Then he just smiled and walked away. I hurried back to my car before I started to cry. On the way back to my sister's house, I started to cry uncontrollably. So much that I had to pull over. I asked myself if this was the life I wanted to continue to live. How is this love? Once I reached my sister's house, I went straight to the guest room and laid on the bed. That night I knew it was the beginning, of the end, of my marriage.

For so long, I had held on to my marriage so tightly, when it had been so clear it was time to let go. I could never find the courage to leave, so I always found reasons to stay. I loved him. I never knew my father, and I wanted our sons to know theirs. I stayed for the security. He was an excellent provider, and I believed in him, and I thought he believed in me. I stayed because I felt worthless, and I felt as though no other man would want me. I felt like I deserved to be treated this way. I had stayed out of fear. Fear of having to start over. Fear of not knowing if I would be able to make it on my own. I stayed because I didn't believe in myself. I stayed because there were some good times in our marriage where I really felt loved and appreciated. When I married my husband, I was already a broken person. I came into our relationship with baggage, and I had no self-worth because I didn't love myself. I felt deserving of the way he treated me.

Over the years, I had started to resent our relationship. Years ago, when we lived in Beaumont, I felt myself mentally checking out of our marriage. I went through the motions. I noticed that it was becoming hard for me to show and give love to someone who, at times, could be so hateful and so mean. I no longer cared about his thoughts, and it became impossible to even hold a conversation with my husband. It was like we were two strangers living in the same house. I was growing tired of self-blaming myself after every fight or argument. As I laid there in bed, I came to the realization that I had stayed in this manipulative and abusive relationship because it was familiar to me. I was willing to let this relationship kill me because I was more afraid of the unfamiliar.

Two weeks later I was back at home.

CHAPTER 9

SURRENDER

"The strongest position you can be in is in complete surrender."

—UNKNOWN

Growing up in Kansas City, church life was an essential part of my life. I was in the youth choir, on the usher board, and I had to recite Easter speeches. With my uncle being the pastor of the church, I had no choice but to participate in everything. There was a time when I knew all the books of the bible, and I could repeat bible verses without a second thought. I even played church with my dolls down in the basement. I said my prayers every morning, each time I ate and before bed every night. I'd always ask my uncle how God could be everywhere all the time and he would explain that God is omnipresent, which meant God is present with His whole self at all times. Still confused, I'd just say okay, but a few days later, I'd asked the same question again. Some nights, I tried to imagine what God really looked like. Did He look like the picture my aunt had hanging downstairs in the living room? A man with pale skin, blue eyes and blonde hair. Or did he look like the man described in the books in my uncle's office? A man with skin dark as mine and with hair like wool.

Even though I had all of these questions, I believed God was real. God was somehow always included in conversations between my aunt and uncle. They talked about Him like He was sitting there on the front porch with us. They always gave praise and thanks to Him and because they believed. I believed.

But as I got older, I drifted away from my faith and the Church. God was no longer a constant presence in my life. We didn't attend church regularly when I lived in Dallas with my mother. Once I married, God wasn't included in conversations between my husband and I like He was with my aunt and uncle. Over time, and with the pressures of life, God just became a distant thought in my mind. Sundays became a day of rest; Days where I slept in late and laid around the house all day. All those bible scriptures I knew when I was younger, I could no longer remember. I had no prayer life. Basically, I made no time for God. I was busy trying to meet the standards of people who supposedly loved me. I felt as though my life was filled with so many failures and disappointments that God didn't want anything to do with me. If I was failing to meet the expectations of other people, I'd never be able to meet God's standards. But now, with all the uncertainties in my marriage, with the suicidal thoughts that kept resurfacing in my mind; I found myself awake in bed at night thinking about God. I even started attending churches, but I felt out of place. So I just brushed off those feelings and told myself God didn't have time for a messed up person like me. But something inside of me just would not let it rest. It was all I thought about each night before I drifted off to sleep.

One morning while driving to work, I asked myself if this was the life God planned for me. Ever since our move to Dallas, it seemed as though everything had gotten worse instead of better. My husband blamed me for everything that was going wrong in our marriage. It was my fault that he got arrested, had to get an attorney and report to a bail bondsman every week. Even though the case was dismissed, because I refused to testify against him, my husband still carried hostility towards me. There was so much tension in the house. We hardly spoke to one another. He spent a lot of time in his office on his computer. He told me he was working, but I knew that was where he hid any liquor he didn't want me to know about. The only time he wanted to talk was when he was drunk. The only thing he wanted to talk about was his arrest. He wanted to know everything I told the police. In his mind, he felt justified for beating me. Why couldn't he understand that his actions got him arrested. It infuriated me that all he thought about was himself. I felt as though he didn't have any remorse for what he had done. He never once apologized. He never once asked me how I felt. A few times, I asked if he would attend some type of counseling, but he always said no. He made it clear he was not going to attend any anger management classes. He told me over and over that he did not have a problem. I was the one with the problem because I did not know how to obey him.

After a weekend of arguing again over him being arrested, which led to me leaving and staying in a hotel for a night; I once again suggested counseling. This time, to my surprise, he agreed. But he told me he wanted to choose the counselor we saw. He wanted to see a woman counselor because he would be more comfortable talking to a woman. But I knew why he wanted a woman counselor, so he could have control. My husband was very charismatic, and he knew how to talk to people, especially women. Even though I knew all of this, I agreed.

We started going to counseling once a week. In those sessions, my husband only wanted to talk about me. He only wanted to point out my flaws, which frustrated me. I knew I wasn't perfect, but neither was he. Every time the counselor wanted to talk about him, he'd always directed the discussion back to me and my flaws. After a few sessions, the counselor figured out what my husband was doing. One night in our session, the counselor became adamant that my husband needed to take some responsibility for his actions. I could tell that my husband became annoyed, and he didn't like that she stood up to him. He fired right back at her, telling her he was not at fault for anything. He simply told her that he was perfect, and he was not the problem in our marriage. I was. The counselor calmly told him he was wrong. We were both at fault and until he accepted his flaws, our marriage would always be incomplete. After she said that, my husband shut down and didn't want to continue the session. When we left, my husband told me we were never going back. He told me she was fake and our marriage was fine as long as I obeyed. I was devastated and at my lowest emotionally. If he didn't want to continue counseling, I didn't know what else to do. We never went back to counseling after that day.

That Saturday, after a long run, I came back to an empty house. My husband was not there, and I was relieved. He was probably off somewhere drinking with some of his friends. I didn't even become upset or worried about him not being there; I was glad to have the house all to myself. I was glad to have a moment of peace. I went into our bedroom and started to run a bath. I got undressed and got into the tub, and closed my eyes.

For the past month since the arrest, suicidal thoughts had entered my mind once again and I contemplated ending my life. I felt as though it was the only way I could be at peace. I was tired of living this life. I was hurting and I wanted out of it. I disliked the woman I had become. I saw myself as a coward. I couldn't even stand to look at myself in the mirror. After laying in the tub for about an hour lost in my thoughts, I finally came back to reality. I bathed, put on my sleep clothes, got in bed and cried myself to sleep. The next morning when I woke up, my husband was asleep beside me. I didn't remember him coming home. I laid in bed for a few more minutes, then got up, got dressed and went into the T.V. room. The whole day I walked around the house feeling numb. That Sunday was a blur, with me lost in my thoughts and just going through the motions. I thought about what my high school literature teacher told me many years ago about having a purpose. Here I was in my forties in a hopeless marriage, and I still didn't know what that purpose was, but I felt as though that purpose was keeping me alive.

Since we were no longer attending counseling, every conversation with my husband had become an interrogation. "Where have you been? Why did it take you so long to come home? Who are you talking to?" I detested being around him. As soon as I'd get home from work, I'd change my clothes and go for a run, just to avoid talking to him. Every time I'd hear a beer bottle open, my insides would knot up. I hated the weekends and holidays because on those days he'd binge drink. To calm my nerves, I'd keep comfort foods around the house to snack on. Then, after I ate, I'd be so disgusted with myself I'd go into the bathroom and make myself vomit. I was self-destructing.

Whenever I'd see my cousin, she would always invite me to church, but I would never go, instead I would make up some excuse to get out of going. I finally ran out of excuses and I agreed to go with her. That Sunday, as we drove up to the church, I could tell it was a large church with a large congregation. That kind of turned me off because I had always heard that when a church is large, the members often feel disconnected. From the moment I entered the building, I didn't get that feeling at all. The people were very friendly and welcoming. They greeted me with smiles and hugs. It was inviting. Once the service started, the music was soothing and it calmed my soul. When the pastor got up to preach, it reminded me a lot of my uncle's preaching. It was real; it was clear and I could relate. I left that church feeling revitalized. The next Sunday I attended and again I left feeling refreshed. I attended a few more Sundays and each time I left with the same energized feeling. I was hooked. Church soon became my refuge. I looked forward to Sundays; it was my escape from the insanity at home. Even if it was just a few hours of calmness and peace, I wanted it. No matter what happened the night before, I made sure I got up and attended every Sunday.

One particular Saturday started out as a normal day. I got up, went for my run, came back and started cleaning the house. My husband spent the morning working out in the yard and cleaning the cars. He had been drinking beer most of the day. That evening we went to get some fast food and rented some DVD's. I can't remember the name of the movies we rented, but I do remember it was funny and we could not stop laughing. He kept going into the kitchen and I thought he was getting another beer, but I soon realized he had traded beer for shots of whiskey. All of the sudden I felt that uneasy feeling, and I hoped he'd just fall asleep. But he didn't. He kept going into the kitchen and refilling his glass. I tried to pretend that I didn't notice what he was doing, so I just kept watching the movie.

When I finally glanced over at him, I noticed his demeanor had changed, and he couldn't keep still in his chair. When I looked at his face, I saw that his eyes had turned black, and he had this eerie expression on his face. I soon realized that I was no longer looking at my husband. I was looking at "Butch", and once "Butch" surfaced, I knew it was going to be a long night.

Once he saw me looking at him, he instantly started with the verbal abuse. We argued most of the night and into the early morning. He wanted to argue about everything. He wanted to argue about things from my past. Things that happened before we were married when I was still a teenager.

In his drunken rage, he brought up how he still loved me, even though I was fat and terrible in bed. He told me I should be grateful that he wanted to be with someone like me because he could do so much better. He wanted me to admit that I had an affair with my cousin. And when I told him there was no affair with my cousin or anyone else, it just made him angrier. He asked to look through my phone, so I let him. He saw and read a text message between me and my sister. I had shared with her that my son was thinking about proposing to his girlfriend. When my husband saw this text he threw my phone into the wall with such force that it made a hole in the wall.

My husband didn't like my sister at all, and it angered him that I had a relationship with her. He kept going on and on with his interrogation. I continued to answer his questions and still he didn't like my answers. He was drunk, and he wanted to argue. I sat on the couch in fear, wondering when and if this was going to get physical, but he never once tried to hit me. He got up from his chair and went outside. While he was outside I thought about leaving, but before I could get my things, he came back into the house. He went into our bedroom and spray painted a big white question mark on the wall in our bedroom. He told me he was going to leave this question mark on the wall until I answered all of his questions. I stared at that question mark on our bedroom wall and I felt hopeless and trapped. I had answered his questions. I sat there emotionally drained. I didn't know what else to do. I didn't know what he wanted me to say. I was so tired of being treated this way. I had done everything to prove my love to this man. I had done everything he asked me to do. Finally, after hours of him ranting over and over about how I was a worthless welfare whore and a tramp, he went into the T.V. room and turned up the stereo really loud. I just sat in our room staring at the big white question mark on the wall. I couldn't even cry; I was all cried out. I kept waiting for him to come back into the room but he never did, and I was too afraid to come out. Finally, around two or three am, he turned off the music. A little while after, I went into the T.V. room and saw he had fallen asleep. I never went to sleep. I just sat in our room staring at the wall. Around six in the morning, I got dressed and left for church before he woke up.

Upon my arrival at church, I noticed that my sister and my cousin had not arrived. I went and sat where we always sat and waited for them. Normally we all would meet up and after service we'd go and eat breakfast. But this Sunday they never showed up and I sat there alone. I was glad they were not there because if they were, they would have seen the despair and desperation on my face. Deep down inside, I knew my marriage was coming to an end, and I didn't know how to save it. To be honest, I didn't want to. I just knew I had endured all I could. The night before had really taken a toll. I was exhausted. This way of life was no longer the life I wanted to live. My home life had become unbearable. I was fed up with the countless accusations. I could no longer tolerate the drinking. The verbal and physical attacks had drained me mentally. I was tired of feeling unloved and unwanted.

Tired of the uneasiness I felt every day not knowing who I was coming home to. Our home did not feel like a home anymore. To me, it felt like a war zone.

That Sunday, as I sat in church, I just let the tears stream down my face. A lady sitting behind me handed me a Kleenex and patted me on the back. If she only knew, my tears were not tears of hope, but tears of despair. I was unable to focus on the sermon, nor was I following what the choir was singing. I just kept thinking about what I was going to do once church was over, because I didn't want to go home. I knew my husband would be awake. I knew when I got home from church he would want to have sex. I got a sick feeling just thinking about him touching me after everything that had happened the night before. But I knew I couldn't say no. It was not an option. If I said no, it would just start another argument, which I could not mentally or emotionally handle. So, I would comply with what he wanted just to keep the peace. This was the blueprint of our marriage.

In that moment at church with tears flowing from my eyes and feeling desperate, I said to God, "Here I am with all my stuff, please help me." That is all I said. I wanted help from someone, from somewhere. I knew I needed some guidance and instructions on what to do with my life. After I said that prayer, the pastor opened the doors of the church, which meant that anyone who wanted to join could do so during this time. I stood up and stepped out of the aisle and that day, I joined the church. I didn't know what to expect, but I didn't know where else to turn. I was at my lowest. My suicidal thoughts were becoming more powerful every day, and I didn't know how much longer I could hold off the desire to follow through and kill myself.

Since I had been coming to church, I liked the way I felt when I was there and the way I felt when I left. So I surrendered. I needed God to save me from myself. I was greeted with a hug by a member, who led me out of the sanctuary. We went into the meeting room, where we sat down and talked about the plan of salvation. The person enrolling me in church asked if I knew what that meant. I replied yes, I knew what it meant. The plan of salvation includes the creation, the fall and the atonement of Jesus Christ. I knew this plan was created by God. To receive salvation, I knew I had to admit to God and to myself that I was a sinner. I needed to confess that Jesus Christ is my Savior and that he died to pay the price for my sins. I sat there for a moment and took in everything I just said. Was I ready to commit? Was I ready to surrender my fears, my self-doubt and my insecurities to God? Was I ready to be vulnerable? Would God even want a relationship with me?

I knew I needed a change, so I completed a membership card and signed up for new member's class. As I walked out of church that day, I felt like a heavy load had been lifted. I didn't feel alone anymore. I went home that day, and I didn't say a word to my husband about what I had done. I wasn't going to allow him to take away this peaceful feeling I felt. It was mine to keep. Surprisingly, we didn't talk much that day. We stayed out of each other's way, and I was glad. He stayed in the T.V. room, and I stayed in the bedroom. I only came out to get something to eat. That evening I slept peacefully; something I had not done in a long time. I don't even remember when my husband came to bed. I only remember when I woke up the next day and found him next to me.

Over the next couple of months, I attended bible study and other church events. I wanted to know about my church village. I was full of so many anxieties. Even though I knew I was supposed to be surrendering the person I was and becoming a new person in Christ, I was still struggling to let go of some of my old traits, like the desire to be liked, to be seen as a nice person, and the need to accommodate. But God knew exactly what He was doing when He led me to this group of believers. This church reminded me of my childhood at my uncle's church, but only now I was an adult, and I was experiencing things through adult eyes. No matter how my day was going, I knew once I was around my new church family, everything would be alright. I knew my cup would be filled and running over when I left. Everyone offered unconditional love. From the time I entered the doors of the church, there were endless hugs and warm smiles welcoming me. Some of the people even knew me by name, which made me feel like I belonged. This unconditional love was also true when it came to our pastor. You could tell he loved people just by how approachable he was. He knew everyone by name, and he had this way of making you feel at ease in his presence. He was genuine and his generosity knew no limits. He was straightforward, confident, and comfortable with who he was. He didn't have a problem sharing that he was not perfect, and that he was human, just like us. I found this to be refreshing and genuine. Since I was living an illusion of a life, afraid for anyone to know my reality, I could only dream about being that secure with who I was. He LOVED God and it showed. The church was filled with phenomenal preachers and teachers who shared the word so effortlessly that anyone could relate.

The more I attended church, the more I wanted to share about my experience with my husband. I don't know why, I just felt compelled to talk about the joy I felt each time I went. I'd share what I learned in bible study or what the pastor talked about in Sunday service. But as I suspected, my husband soon became annoyed with me attending church. He became upset about the time I was spending there. He told me I was changing. I just ignored him and kept going. One Friday evening, we got into a heated argument about me going to church, and he wanted to know why I never invited him to church. Church was my haven, and I wanted to keep it to myself. I knew it was wrong, but it was the only place where I experienced peace. I knew once my husband went, and if he didn't like it, he'd find a way to make me stop going. I reluctantly invited him because it was the right thing to do. Deep down inside, some part of me thought maybe he'd see how kind everyone was and he'd understand why I enjoyed going. My husband's response to me was he doesn't do church. Church was fake. Church was filled with a bunch of fake people and all they wanted from you was your money. I just looked at him and thought, what was the point of this argument if he didn't care about going. I didn't care what he said; I was not going to stop going. I wasn't going to allow him to take away the secure feeling I felt each time I went.

My husband saw that no matter what he said about church, I was still going to go, so he got up one Sunday and went with me. A part of me was suspicious. Why was he coming? When we arrived, we met up with my sister and my cousin. They both looked surprised to see him. After service, we all went and had breakfast. It was awkward, because both my sister and cousin were still angry with my husband, because of what they knew about the abuse. They loved and supported me and my decision to stay in my marriage, so they didn't say anything.

On the way home, I asked my husband what he thought about the church service, and he said he enjoyed it. I felt relieved. I had already made up my mind that no matter what he said, I wasn't going to stop going. That Wednesday he went with me to bible study. Then that next Sunday morning, he got up and went with me again to service. I was so elated. I thought that maybe this would be our break-through. I bought my husband a Bible and I had his name inscribed on it. I noticed that he started reading it daily and this made me really happy. We were both young when we married, and we had to figure out a lot of things on our own, and maybe now with the both of us going to church and studying the Word we could heal and become one.

The more I attended church, the more I started to understand the relationship my aunt and uncle had with God. The relationship they had instilled in me as a young girl. The relationship I walked away from as an adult. But now I had embarked on this journey to renew my relationship; I wanted to know more about God. I wanted to rekindle our relationship. I wanted to know more about the God who loved me so much that He gave His life for my sins. The more I studied, God's Word began to fill an empty void that was inside of me. I started to feel whole. I hadn't felt this way since I was a little girl living in Kansas City, Mo. My husband was right, I was changing. I started to see myself the way God saw me, and I started to see that my marriage was filled with issues. Yes, my husband was a good provider. I didn't want anything material, but my marriage lacked emotional support. The way he treated me was disrespectful. His dogmatic behavior dominated our marriage. The abuse I experienced in my marriage was my husband's way of controlling me. He saw me as his property and not as his wife. Being involved in church again, I was slowly learning to see myself the way God saw me. It wasn't long before I soon found the courage to stand up to my husband. I started to voice how I felt about his drinking and the way he treated me when he was drunk. My husband didn't like that I was finding my voice, and he didn't like my newfound boldness. Each time I'd stand up to him, it would anger him. At times he'd tried to regain control by twisting scripture, name calling and chastising me. Like a roaring lion, he'd let me know he was the man, and I was supposed to bow down and submit. But I never once let his antics deter me. Every day I continued to study, and I prayed for guidance. I never stopped going to church. The strength I had found in God was overwhelming, and I was no longer afraid of what my husband would do. For the first time in a long time, I felt God's presence. He was with me and I felt His love.

Slowly, I became a part of my church village. I started volunteering for events held at the church. It felt liberating to be around people who would listen without judgement. I began to form relationships with women and men who would mentor and guide me. People that would help me to see my worth. In a village, everybody looks out for each other. No matter what your flaws are. You are a part of the village and the people of the village love you unconditionally.

I had found my village.

CHAPTER 10

TODAY WAS THE DAY

"Walking through the Red Sea does not require
extra strength but complete faith."

—UNKNOWN

Being involved in church and being around encouraging people was good for my self-confidence. We were all seeking a relationship with God. We were all imperfect and broken. Any time spent with my church village was good for my soul. It was like the empty parts of me were being filled with love and acceptance. I was starting to feel whole. With those feelings of wholeness, a change came over me. I started to behave in a way that put my inner peace as my main priority. On my runs, I stopped listening to music and started listening to podcasts on how to love myself. I posted affirmations all over my mirror in my dressing room. Affirmations on self-love, self-worth and on being courageous. I bought books on faith, love, and respect. I started attending a women's ministry class at my church that focused on teaching me to see myself the way God saw me. I met women in this group who began to mentor and guide me in my Christian walk. My prayer life became real and important to me.

I started to pray without ceasing. I prayed in the morning, in my car, on my runs and every time I entered our home. During my prayers, I felt a stillness and calmness that would just take my breath away. I could truly feel the presence of God. I only read books that encouraged and empowered me. This new empowerment motivated me to want to look my best physically. I wanted my outward appearance to mimic the way I had started to feel on the inside. So, I started setting goals for myself to get in better shape. Besides running, I added yoga and weight training. I challenged myself mentally by entering and running in half marathons. I was determined to see myself the way that God saw me. I was on a mission to find and know my worth. I was on a mission to show myself love.

While I was on a quest to discover myself, I felt as though my husband was on a quest to keep me under his control. He still attended church, but at home, nothing had changed. There were still the drinking binges with the verbal attacks and the accusations of me having affairs. But every Sunday morning, we got up and went to church and pretended to be the perfect couple. I was growing tired of this masquerade. Our marriage was unhealthy, and I finally recognized that it wasn't all my husband's fault. I had allowed a lot of the abuse I endured. Most of my life I looked to others for my worth, to show me how to love. I looked to the others to tell me I was beautiful and wanted. I needed to be appreciated by others so badly, and I yearned for the acceptances of others. When I didn't receive it, I would try hard to prove to them I was worthy of having it. I was incapable of seeing my worth through my own eyes and my husband knew this.

One evening while watching the news, the reporter talked about an abusive relationship that turned deadly. A man shot and killed his girlfriend and her seventeen-year-old daughter in Dallas and then traveled to the nearby city of DeSoto and killed his estranged wife and her twenty-eight-year-old daughter. As I watched this story, a chill came over me. I felt as though I knew the women that were killed. I did not need to meet them personally but I was living their story. The story of abuse. That Sunday in church, my Pastor made an announcement that our church would hold funeral services for the mother and daughter that lived in DeSoto. On the day of the funeral, I took an early lunch and attended the service. As I sat there, I stared at them as they lay in their coffins, and I cried. I cried because they were so young. I cried because they died a senseless death. I cried because deep down inside of me I knew that one day I'd be the one laying in a coffin if I didn't make changes.

Over the next couple of months, it seemed like every week there was a story on the news about domestic violence. As I watched these stories and listened to the families talk about their loved ones that were killed, I wondered if their families knew about the abuse. Or if the women were protecting their abuser and living a charade like I was. Being in an abusive relationship leaves a person feeling isolated. Even when others know about the abuse, they don't want to get involved, so they stay silent. I had seen stories before on domestic violence, but now for some reason, these stories haunted me. Each time I read about or watched a news report about domestic violence, I'd lay in bed at night thinking about the victims. I don't know what it was, but for the first time in my life, I felt as though my life mattered. My happiness mattered. I started to think seriously about asking my husband for a divorce. In my mind there was no hope for our marriage, and counseling was pointless because in my husband's eyes he was not the problem I was. I was the reason for his drinking. I was the reason for his verbal outburst. Each time he had hit me, it was my fault. I knew it was time I found the courage to have the tough conversation. The conversation about ending our marriage.

One Thursday I came home from work and found my husband in his normal place:in his office on his computer, pretending to be working. I said hello and went into our bedroom to change out of my work clothes. I wasn't feeling well and I just wanted to lay down. Before I could nod off, I looked up and saw him standing at the door, staring at me. Instantly, I put my guard up and sat up in bed because I knew the look on his face. I had seen it so many times in our marriage. It was "Butch". He stared at me a little longer, and then he turned and walked away. I knew that tonight was going to be a long night. Something inside of me told me to get up, get dressed, and leave. Something inside of me said *Today was the day*. So, I got up and got dressed. I heard him come back down the hall. I looked up and he was standing at the door. Right away, "Butch" started with the accusations. This time, I was having an affair with someone at my church.

I didn't say a word, I just looked at him. I always wondered when these accusations would start. My husband had seen how much I enjoyed going to church. He saw how involved I was becoming and he didn't like it. Anytime he felt threatened or insecure about something I was doing or by someone I was in a friendship with, he'd always accuse me of having an affair. He had done this in San Diego, Corpus Christi, Hawaii, Great Lakes and in Beaumont. This had been our entire marriage. Twenty-six years of me doing whatever it took to please him. I ended friendships. I even walked away from jobs. I gave my whole being to this marriage, so much so that I had become this woman who was lifeless on the inside. So, as my husband turned and left the room again, I thought to myself, *Today was the day*.

I could hear my husband calling me a whore, a tramp, a liar, and everything else he could think of as he walked into the next room. I then heard my husband go into the kitchen. Most likely to fix himself a drink. I knew all too well what was going to happen next. It was going to be a long night of arguing with verbal and physical attacks. This would go on for hours into the early morning. Then once he grew tired of hearing himself talk, he'd want to have sex and I better not resist. During sex, he'd profess how much he loved me. I'd just lie there exhausted from defending myself and holding my breath so I could not smell the stank liquor seeping through his pores, waiting for it to be over. Once it was over and he had passed out, I'd go take a shower and cry in secret. The next day we'd wake up and act like nothing happened. I'd spend the whole day tormenting myself trying to figure out what I had done to deserve this. I'd spend the day waiting for an apology I'd never get.

But today something was different. I told myself I was done with this life. I was tired. I was broken. I wanted to be free. I no longer wanted to be a puppet going through the motions to keep the peace. For so long, I wanted to leave, but I had been afraid, afraid of the unknown. This had been my life for twenty-six years. I was afraid of what people would think. What would my kids say? But deep down inside, I knew if I stayed in this relationship, I would end up dead. Either my husband was going to kill me, or I was going to kill myself.

Today was the day I told myself again. I went into my closet and put on my shoes. I dared myself to do it, to leave. Many times before I said *Today was the day* that I was going to leave, but I always coward out and stayed. And the times I did leave, I always came back. So why was today different? I really don't know why. I just knew that for me to stay here any longer was far more frightening than it was for me to leave. I called my sister, grabbed my purse and I started walking towards the garage to my car. My husband saw me going towards the garage and he called me a slut and told me to go ahead. "You will be back," he said. But I knew this time I wasn't coming back. I knew *Today was the day*. He followed me to the garage, and I kept waiting for him to hit me or grab me, but not once did he try to stop me. It felt so surreal. He asked for the door key and the garage door opener, and I handed both items to him. He kept on with the verbal attacks, but I never said a word because the only thought in my head was *Today was the day*. I got in my car and backed out of the garage. As I drove away, I didn't cry. I felt relieved. *Today was the day*. I had decided I was going to walk with God even though I didn't understand or know where He was going to take me. *Today was the day*. I was going to trust and believe. Once I got to my sister's house, I told her what was going on, and she told me I could stay as long as I needed.

In bed that night, I thought about how strange it was that I was just able to leave. Any other time, my husband would have been all over me, and I would have never made it out of the bedroom. It was like I was protected. I felt so calm, and I wasn't scared at all. I thought about the story in the Bible about Moses and the Israelites. I thought about how calm Moses had stayed and how he trusted God. I thought about how when the Israelites came to the Red Sea, they wondered how they would get across to the other side to escape from Pharaoh. I thought about how God parted the sea so they could get across. Then I smiled and thought about how God was with me when I left. He had parted the sea, so I could cross. Then I turned over and went to sleep. For the first time in a long time, a feeling of peace came over me. I didn't know what the future held, but I told myself I was ready for the journey.

CHAPTER 11

THE WHISPER

"To hear God's voice you must turn down the world's volume."

–Unknown

It had been about three months since I left my husband and moved in with my sister. I was grateful to my sister for giving me a place of refuge. She was doing everything she could to make me feel safe and at ease. Depending on who arrived home first from work, one of us would cook dinner. Some Saturdays we would hang out together and do sister stuff. We'd go and get our eyebrows threaded, or we'd go get manicures and pedicures. On Sundays after church, we would find a Soul Food restaurant to eat at. Some days, we would hibernate and stay inside in our pajamas, talking and watching movies all day. Even though I enjoyed spending time with her, I still at times would find myself deep in thought about leaving the only life I had known since my adulthood.

To quiet these thoughts, I stayed busy with work, therapy, and spending time at the gym. Trying hard not to dwell on all the feelings of uncertainty I was experiencing. I was in my forties, and here I was, starting my life over. Some nights I'd lay in bed and look at all the boxes that held everything I owned stacked in the corner of my sister's guest bedroom. That was all I had to show for twenty-six years of marriage. One night while I stared at those boxes I heard a voice say, *"But you have your life."* Yes, I was thankful to be alive and excited about my newfound freedom, and I was also grateful for all the people God was continuously bringing into my life, but I was having a hard time adjusting to it all and finding my way. My finances were depleted. Everything I had was going to my attorney and towards therapy. The whole divorce process was becoming ugly and debilitating. My husband wasted no time with the hateful text messages and threatening phone calls. A constant reminder to me of how worthless I felt. I tried really hard to ignore them. I knew he was angry, and since he couldn't take his rage out on me physically, and in person, he was going to do it verbally and emotionally. I thought eventually he'd stop and leave me alone, but that was not the case.

One Tuesday night after my sister and I went to bed, my husband showed up at her house. My sister came into my room and woke me up to tell me that my husband was on her cell phone and he was telling her he was parked outside her house and he wanted to speak with me. I told my sister to hang up. He called back again, and this time I answered the phone. He instantly went into a rant saying I was not at my sister's but instead out with a man. I told him I was inside, but I was not coming out. He told me to come outside so we could talk, and that if I was there I should come outside and prove it. I told him he should go home because I wasn't coming out, and I was going to call the police if he didn't leave.

When he refused to leave, my sister called the police, and we waited inside until they came. Once the police came, I could see his whole demeanor changed. He was no longer talking loud or threatening not to leave. He became silent and compliant with the officers, and he acted as though he wasn't doing anything wrong. I could see, through the window, one of the officers talking to him while leading him across the street. The other officer came up to the house and knocked on the door.

When my sister opened the door he asked if we were okay. We said yes, and I explained to the officer that I had left my husband and was in the process of filing for a divorce. I told him about how my husband had been harassing me with endless text messages and numerous phone calls. I asked what I could do to stop the harassment. The officer explained to me that I needed to go down to the police station and see about filing a restraining order. He went on to say that since no one was physically hurt from this incident all they could do was ask my husband to leave; they could not arrest him. As I stood there, I could see my husband across the street still talking with the other officer but I could not hear what was being said. A few moments later I saw him get into his car and drive away.

Once the police left, I went back into the house, apologized to my sister and went back into my room. I didn't want to talk about what happened. I felt embarrassed, helpless and terrified. I couldn't go to sleep because I worried that he would come back. I worried about what would happen if he did. I even thought about going to a Women's Shelter; I didn't want to have to worry about my sister's safety. I didn't want to put her in any harm. I felt so alone. I spent the rest of the night tossing and turning trying to quiet my mind, until I heard a voice that said, *"You're not alone",* this voice comforted me and finally I drifted off to sleep.

The next day I went to the police precinct to file a complaint and to see what my options were, but I soon learned from the officer on duty that my husband could make all the verbal threats he wanted, until he physically harmed me again, there wasn't much they could do to protect me. Hearing the police officer say these things infuriated me. I stood there thinking to myself that if the police could not protect me or help me then who could? As I walked out of the Police Precinct to my car, I understood how all those women felt in the articles I had read on domestic violence. In those stories, they had left their abuser only to return because they could not get any protection which made them feel helpless. Driving away from the precinct I realized that yes I had left my marriage, but I was not free and my husband still had control. Just the thought of this made me angrier. I knew my husband would never stop with the harassment and there was nothing I could do legally.

Through therapy I learned my husband was a narcissist and they thrive on being in control. Narcissists are good at blaming and deflecting, never taking responsibility for anything unless it makes them look superior. My therapist explained to me that leaving my husband was going to be tough because I had fed his ego for so many years. And since I chose to leave, he was going to be whatever it took to punish me and make me feel guilty for leaving.   In the days following this incident, my husband continued with the threats, the false promises and the pleas for reconciliation. Every time he'd get drunk he found a way to let me know how he felt about me leaving. I knew I'd have to take extreme measures to stop his insanity. If I didn't, I'd forever be in his bondage. I'd forever be looking over my shoulder worried about running into him.

I thought about moving away to another city and starting over: a new place, a new beginning. I started thinking about where I wanted to go, and then I heard a voice that said, *"Moving away will not free you."* What does that mean? I thought. That night I prayed to God for clarity, because moving seemed like the perfect thing to do. I woke up the next day, still unsure about what to do. I got dressed and drove to my weekly therapy session. I started therapy as soon as I left my husband because I needed someone to talk to. Someone who would not judge. Someone who would not gossip. Someone I could trust.

That day in therapy I discussed with my therapist my thoughts about leaving Dallas. I told her about everything that happened that week with my husband showing up at my sister's house. I explained what the police told me and how there wasn't much they could do to protect me unless my husband assaulted me physically. I told her I felt it was best I leave Dallas and start over somewhere else. After I was done talking, my therapist told me she didn't think leaving was a good idea. She asked if I really wanted to start over somewhere else, or if I wanted to leave because I was afraid: afraid that he would harm me or afraid he'd convince me to come back. I didn't know how to answer her questions. I still had a lot of conflicted feelings about my marriage. Deep down inside I knew I had done the right thing by leaving, but a part of me missed my husband and wanted to go back to him. My marriage had been my whole life. I left therapy that day angry with myself and upset with my therapist. I wanted her to give me all the answers, but that's not what happened. She had shown me how dysfunctional I truly was.

For some reason, in my mind, I truly thought I was deserving of the abuse I endured in my marriage. I sat in the parking lot and cried. I thought to myself, *will I ever have peace?* That next week I walked around preoccupied. I was constantly looking over my shoulder, always wondering if my husband was going to show up again at my sister's or at my job. What was I going to do if he did? I changed up my hours at my accounting job, just in case he did show up. I changed the places I went for my runs, just in case he showed up there. I did everything I could do to change up my routine. On my runs, I'd run until I was exhausted. I wanted to be so tired at night that all I could do was go to sleep and not have to worry about my circumstances. Most of all I was tired of staring at those damn boxes in the corner and feeling sorry for myself.

One day while on my lunch break, I started surfing the internet to fill the time, like I always did. I surfed topics on surviving domestic violence. I clicked on a link that took me to a page for a women's shelter. I read through the home page, and saw a link at the bottom of the page asking for volunteers. I clicked on the link and after some thought, I decided to sign up. In my mind this is something I could do to fill up some time and maybe I could learn from the other women. A couple of weeks after completing the form, I was invited to attend a one on one meeting with the director. Upon arrival, she showed me around the facility and then we went into her office to finish the interview. Her first question to me was about why I wanted to become a volunteer. I shared with her how I had been in an abusive marriage and how I felt as though I could connect with the other women at the shelter.

For about 30 minutes, we talked and she explained the rules and guidelines. For example, I was not allowed to discuss my religious beliefs because there were women in the shelter whose beliefs were different from mine. Since I was not a licensed counselor, I'd only be able to listen to the women and be encouraging. I was never to give advice. She then gave me a packet that needed to be completed. I was to provide 3 references she could contact to talk with about my character. A week later, I got a call letting me know that everything checked out and the director asked me what day I could start.

On my first day, one of the other volunteers showed me where I would be working. For the first month, I would be working at the front desk where people had to sign in and out of the shelter. No one at the shelter, besides the director, knew my story. It was comforting being around other women whose life was similar to mine. I could relate to their stories. I'd sit and listen to the women talk about the abuse they had endured. I'd give them words of encouragement, all the while keeping my story a secret. Everyone at the shelter saw me as this person who had it all together, but if they only knew how lost I was. I was good at masquerading, and what they saw was a façade. They didn't know while I was encouraging them; I was also trying to encourage myself.

One Friday evening I left the shelter and while I was driving back to my sister's house, I heard a voice that said, *"How long are you going to keep wearing the mask?"* I knew instantly what that meant. I immediately started to feel guilty about keeping my secret. Maybe I wasn't ready to be a volunteer, I thought. I mean, how could I keep going to this place and listening to these women and being a voice of hope, when I was experiencing the same fears these women had. I was just as afraid as they were. How could I tell them things were going to be okay and that they had made the right decision when I was still conflicted over my own decision to leave?

That night, I came to the conclusion that it was probably best if I stopped volunteering until I was able to walk in my truth. That

Monday, I called and explained to the director my concerns about how I was struggling with my decisions and how I still had a lot of emotional baggage to unpack. We talked for a few minutes and we both agreed I should not come back until I was ready. In my next therapy session, things got intense. My therapist simply told me that I needed to stop playing the victim, stop running and that I started to see myself the way I wanted people to see me. She explained to me that if I wanted respect and wanted to be valued, I needed to value and respect myself. She made me see that my lack of love for myself had caused a lot of the problems in my childhood, my marriage, and other relationships. She explained that if I had loved myself and valued who I was, I would not have allowed my husband and others to treat me so cruelly. After the session, I drove back to my sister's house and took a long hot shower, fell across my bed and thought about the session. It was hard for me to accept what my therapist said, but it was true. I didn't love myself. I honestly didn't know how. I glazed over at all the boxes that were still packed, and I heard a voice that said, *"It's time to unpack."* But I still didn't know if I was ready. I was so comfortable living in my bondage of feeling worthless and unlovable that I wasn't sure if I was ready to let it go.

The next morning when I woke up, I looked at my cell phone and noticed I had numerous text messages from my husband. I read each text and read all the hateful things he said. Not once in those text messages did he apologize. Not once had he asked for my forgiveness. In each text message, he went on with his rant telling me how I was nothing but a slut, a welfare hoe, and how he had this powerful attorney. He made it clear that I wouldn't get a penny of his money. In one text, he said he never should have married me and talked about how he had already replaced me. I became irritated thinking about what the police officer had told me about there being nothing I could do to stop the harassment. After I read the last text message, I decided there was something I could do. I blocked his number. I don't know why it took me so long to do it. I guess some part of me still wanted to work things out. I still loved him. Once I blocked his number, I heard a voice that said, *"Don't worry"*. Hearing this soothed my anxieties and I got out of bed, got dressed, and went to church. During the end of service, my pastor called for altar prayer. Tears started to flow as I walked up to the altar. My pastor started to pray, and as he prayed, I said a silent prayer and asked God for clarity on the things He was saying to me. I knew it was God who told me *I was not alone*. I knew it was Him who said that *moving away would not free me*. It was God who told me it was time to remove the mask and it was time for me to unpack and not to worry. But as I stood there at the altar, I let God know that I was afraid, worried, and felt powerless. I prayed for strength to help me endure, and I prayed for guidance. As I walked back to my seat, that same voice said, *"You can trust me."* I left church that Sunday with a new sense of self and a feeling of love. I walked with my head held high; I felt protected, and I didn't feel ashamed of my story anymore. As I drove away from church, I decided it was time to set up some personal boundaries. I told myself it was time to take control of how I wanted to be treated by other people. My therapist was right; I needed to take my life back. I had taken the first step by blocking my husband's number on my cell phone. I told myself it was time to unpack and release myself from the bondgage of negative thoughts that I kept allowing to destroy the woman I wanted to become. It was time to unpack and get rid of my insecurities and fears. It was time to tear down this vile wall of hopelessness I had built around me.

When I made it back to my sister's house, I changed out of my church clothes, got on the internet and started researching online for classes on self-defense. I also signed up for a concealed weapon class. Since the police would not be able to protect me, I decided it was time I learned to protect myself. After dinner, I started to unpack all the boxes in my room. Once I was done, a sense of relief came over me. Thanks to the voice that constantly assured me that I made the right decision, I was no longer conflicted about my divorce. That week, I signed the divorce papers.

CHAPTER 12

RENOVATION

"Nothing makes a woman more beautiful than the belief that she is beautiful."

—Unknown

For months, after I signed the divorce papers, each night I laid in bed and I mourned my marriage. I thought I'd be married forever. Until death do us part were the vows we took standing in that judge's office twenty-five years before. Just the thought of the relationship being over left me with a feeling of deep loss, guilt, and I was very depressed. I couldn't understand why I could not make my marriage work. I was fully committed. I had done everything that he asked of me. Constantly changing who I was, so I'd be pleasing to his eyes. I replaced my beliefs for his. I often stayed silent when I should have voiced my opinion. One Friday night as I laid in bed unable to fall asleep, thinking about all I had endured. I told myself; I had been married until death do us part, because over the years my ex-husband had drained the life out of me. I was dead mentally and emotionally. During those years, I turned into this pretty doll that was nice to look at but had no soul on the inside.

Once I came to this realization, I took a long exhale, turned over and fell asleep. The next morning, in my prayers, feeling so isolated and lost, I asked God, "What's next for me?"

I waited in silence for a response, but I heard or felt nothing. So, I asked God again "what He had planned for me. I really needed to know. I continued to pray, asking for guidance, all the while hoping God would appear and show me this amazing plan He had for my life. I knew stuff like that only happened in the movies, but I really needed to feel His presence. I mean I was trusting Him, and I was ready to move on with my life. I was ready for a new beginning. I was ready for God to show it to me. I continued going to therapy, and I was slowly becoming more involved in church.

Therapy was helping me cope with all the emotional trauma I was carrying inside, but my self-esteem and the way I saw myself was at its lowest. When I looked at myself in the mirror, I still saw a broken and unhappy woman looking back at me. I saw the little girl who carried the criticism of her mother, and I saw a woman who was struggling to let go of the judgement she received from her ex-husband. I felt as though everyone was watching me and waiting for me to fail. I was in a constant battle with the voices in my head and I was having a hard time freeing myself of my insecurities and fears. I knew it was time to move on, but I didn't know how. For most of my life, I had looked to other people for guidance for love and my self-worth. Now I only had myself to look to, and I felt like none of those things existed in me.

I continued to ask God in my prayers each day what was next for me. I was determined to get an answer. Still, I heard nothing, until one Wednesday night in bible study. That night my teacher taught a lesson on "Our Circle of Influence." He explained to us that if we wanted to have enriched lives, we needed to make sure that we were influenced by people who we respected and trusted. He went on to say that in order to have a healthy circle, we needed to make sure our intentions, communication, values and behaviors were all in line with the people we place around us. We needed to be open, honest, and transparent. The more sincere we were, with ourselves, we would attract the right people and our circle would grow. Next, he told us before we could have astounding horizontal relationships here on earth with people, we first needed to establish a mind-blowing vertical relationship with God. The bible scripture he used was from Proverbs 13:20, **"He who walks with the wise grows wise, but a companion of fools suffers harm."**

Sitting there listening to him, I started to think about my circle of influence. I never really had a lot of friends as a little girl; I was a loner. As a teenager, I substituted my desires for the desires of others so I could fit in. Once I got married, most of my adult relationships revolved around people my ex-husband knew. Now that I had filed for divorce, I realized that those same people I surrounded myself with when I was married didn't really have my best interest at heart. Instead of them being there for me and offering encouragement, I had become the topic of their gossip. Right there in class, I wrote a note to myself stating that I wanted everything that my teacher was talking about. I wanted meaningful relationships with people who were sincere and whose values and behaviors were similar to mine. Also in my notes, I wrote that this moment was a sign from God. He was ready to show me what was next, but first I needed to work on my vertical relationship with Him. Yes, I prayed and attended church and bible study, but that was about it. I wasn't really sharing my faith or my beliefs outside of church with others. I was keeping my Christianity undercover to the outside world. I was too afraid of being judged. In that class, I realized it was time for me to bring my faith and my beliefs forward and into every relationship I had and not worry about being liked or accepted. By doing so, God would lead people to me that would not only lift my spirit, but who would also enrich my life. The class was very informative and I left there inspired and determined to draw closer to God and to create my circle of influence.

First thing I did once I got back to my sister's house was go through my cell phone and delete phone numbers of people who I felt no longer nourished the person I was becoming. As I deleted each number, I felt this dead weight being lifted off of me. In my mind, those people were not concerned with helping me grow. After I was done, my call list was so small that I questioned if I even knew enough people to build a circle of influence. I wondered if I knew one person I could trust and confide in, who I could feel safe with. Someone who would love me unconditionally, and who wasn't afraid to be honest with me.

I felt that some people in my church family met this criteria, who were reaching out to me, and wanting to build a connection. They always offered kind words and hugs each time they saw me, and they seemed to be sincere in their gestures and concerns. But I was still so guarded and untrusting that I was afraid to open up and let them in. I could feel my eyes getting heavy and as I drifted off to sleep that night, I kept thinking about rebuilding my circle. I knew building my circle was important and that I needed to take my time and not rush the process. In the meantime, I dedicated myself to waking up early and spending more time in God's word because that night in bible study I learned that my relationship with Him was more important than any other relationship I could have.

One evening, as I stood in front of the bathroom mirror, massaging some jojoba oil through my locs, I wondered how I would look if I cut my hair. I had been wearing locs for 12 years. I started growing them when I lived in Illinois. As I pulled them back off of my face, I thought, why not? I was already in renovation mode. There were my daily workouts that were revamping my outside appearance, and my weekly therapy sessions were healing my soul. I was renewing my relationship with God and rebuilding my circle of influence. I had been thinking about cutting my hair for some time and I figured a new look would boost my confidence. I continued to stare at myself in the mirror, smiled and told myself it was time for "The Big Cut." My locs were beautiful, I kept them neat, clean and long. Almost down to my butt. People always noticed them and told me how beautiful they were. But staring at those long locs in the mirror reminded me of the woman I was trying to demolish. A woman who was always looking for acceptance and approval from others. They reminded me of the woman I was trying to leave behind. In my mind, each one of my locs carried the weight of my low self-esteem, insecurities, and self-doubt. It was time to get rid of that excess weight. I started to collect pictures of hairstyles I liked. I wanted something short and easy to maintain. After a couple of weeks of looking in hair books and surfing the internet, I found a few that I liked. That Sunday at church, I showed the pictures to my sista-friend at church who was a stylist. A big smile rose up on her face and she looked at me and asked if I was sure I was ready. I told her I was sure and ready, and we scheduled an appointment for the next week.

The whole week before my appointment, every time I looked in the mirror, I tried to imagine how I would look once my locs were gone. On the day of my appointment, I was still undecided on my decision to cut my hair. I found what I thought would be the perfect cut for me. It was short, feminine, and low maintenance. The model portrayed the image I was looking for: confident, strong, and sexy. I arrived early for my appointment. The shop was empty and my sista-friend was ready. Once I was in her chair, she asked again if I was sure, and even though I felt all this nervous energy on the inside, I said yes. She removed the band that was holding my ponytail, parted my hair down the middle, made four sections, grabbed about five or six locs from one section, and began to cut.

As she kept grabbing more locs to cut, I could feel them falling to the floor, and I told myself there goes all of my self-doubt and my insecurities. A few more dropped and I told myself there goes my low self-esteem and my shame. When she was done, I watched her sweep them up and throw them in the trash. I told myself all those burdens I carried for so many years were gone and no longer a part of me. I smiled and thought about how little by little I was constructing myself into the person I saw in my dreams.

Next, my sista-friend began the process of cutting and styling my hair to match the model's hair in the picture. A couple of hours later, she turned the chair around to the big mirror on the wall, and for the first time I saw the new me. At first I didn't recognize the woman that was looking back at me. She looked so beautiful and confident. She looked very sure of who she was. There is a quote that says, "until you see yourself through God's eyes you will always see yourself less than what you are". I stared for a few more minutes, and then I smiled and thought for the first time I was seeing myself the way God saw me. Strong and Confident. On the drive home from the salon, I kept checking myself out in the rearview mirror and smiling. I LOVED the way I looked! I felt totally exposed, flaws and all, and I didn't care who saw me. I couldn't wait to share the new me with the world.

One rainy Saturday after a therapy session, my sister and I decided to stay in and watch movies. After flipping through a few channels, my sister landed on the movie "Enough" with Jennifer Lopez. In this movie she played a woman who met, fell in love and married a rich and powerful man who made her life a living hell. The man she married was controlling and abusive: physically, verbally, and emotionally. After having a child, she decided to leave, but it was not easy. The husband started harassing and stalking her, and she had to go into hiding, moving to different cities and changing her identity. Tired of being afraid and tired of running, she decided to take her life back. A close family member told her about a man who could teach her how to defend herself. This man introduced her to a mixed-martial art style of fighting called Krav Maga. This style of fighting combines boxing, judo, jujitsu, muay thai and aikido. I sat there and watched in amazement. I had never seen fighting like this before. I was in awe at how simple, but effective, the movements were. I watched how this small woman was able to take on and overpower a man twice her size. I wanted those skills! I wanted to be able to fight just like the woman in this movie. I wanted that confidence. I was never going to allow someone to put their hands on me again. I grabbed my computer and googled Krav Maga classes located in my area. After some research,

I found myself in a Krav Maga class two days later. My first thought was that I was in the wrong class. Where were the women? Then I heard a voice inside of me say, *"No this is exactly where you need to be"*, so I stayed. Eventually another woman showed up, and with relief I asked if we could be partners. I was nervous and scared, but I really wanted to be able to protect myself.

The first couple of months I was awful. I had no coordination. My punches were wild and all over the place and I was terrified of being hit. It was hard for me to stay focused and I became terrified when I had to train with a man. They were too aggressive. I'd cower down, cover up, and stop punching when they would attack me. I almost gave up and stopped going around the third month, but one night after class, my instructor walked over to me and said he liked my spirit. I thought to myself, if he only knew my story, but that little bit of encouragement kept me coming back.

Within six months, I noticed that my fears started to decrease and I became more confident in my skills. I didn't care who I trained with, and I wasn't scared to take a punch. A lot of the other instructors started to take notice and started to call me out in class to help demonstrate. Some of them even started to take time out to work with me one on one to help me perfect my skills. The more I went, the more I met amazing people, and a few of them became a part of my circle. They encouraged me and shared their knowledge with me. I no longer felt like an outsider. I felt like a part of the group. This class boosted my confidence. Not only had I learned to fight, I was now in excellent shape and I had learned some important life skills. I learned to stay determined and not to give up. I became aware of everything that went on around me, and I walked with my head up and looked people in their eyes.

One particular instructor made me feel fearless. I met him one Saturday after class. He was one of the instructors there and I overheard him talking to another student about additional training he offered outside of the gym. I later approached him and told him I was interested in some additional training. The first day we trained, I was overwhelmed. His cut-throat, in your face, no mercy approach to teaching took me to the next level. He taught me more than just Krav Maga. In his training, I had to learn to be comfortable in the uncomfortable. We worked on my breathing, which helped me to stay relaxed and focused. He constantly pushed me to be more aggressive, which was a struggle. I was this little girl who grew up to be the woman that never spoke up or defended herself. Now, I was being asked to be the aggressor, the person who sometimes would attack first. This was hard for me to comprehend. This instructor assured me that this type of hard-core *"in your face training"* would make me stronger mentally. It would make me more focused, determined, and not afraid. I wasn't allowed to coward down or quit in his class. I had a hard time adapting at first. Sometimes after class I would be so upset and frustrated with his method of madness, I would cry as I drove back to my sister's house, but I was determined to conquer this fear. Over time, my fighting skills became quite impressive. I was no Ronda Rousey, but I could hold my own. I felt fierce and fearless. I hit like a girl, and I was proud of it.

    2014 had definitely become a year of deconstruction and reconstruction for me. One particular day I decided to take the scenic route on my usual 30 mile commute to work. The traffic was really bad going through downtown Dallas, and the scenic route allowed me to go through Highland Park, one the most elite suburbs in Dallas. There I would see homes being torn down, renovated or updated. Sitting at a red light, I looked over at a house that had been gutted. It was an older home, and I could see where everything on the inside had been torn out and only the shell of the house remained. I thought about all the work and time it was going to take to rebuild that house. A few months later, I drove by the same house and noticed a lot of the renovations had been completed. I could tell that most of the outside was done and from what I could see, some of the inside was almost complete as well, but there was still work to be done. As I kept looking at how beautiful the house was becoming, it made me think about all the renovations that were going on in my life. Since my divorce, I had basically torn down and demolished the woman I used to be. I was currently in the process of rebuilding the woman I wanted to become. The woman I always thought I should be. Little by little and with God's guidance, I was removing all the critics and the naysayers in my life. I was building a circle of influence filled with people from my church and even some from my gym who had my best interest at heart who wanted to see me grow. I had totally changed the way I looked. My new short cut totally exposed me and awakened me on the inside.

For the first time in a long time, I felt beautiful, empowered, disciplined, and confident. I was losing the weight of my insecurities. I nourished my soul daily with devotion, prayer, and meditation. All of these self-renovations were helping me to build a strong and solid foundation. I was slowly starting to like and love the person I saw in the mirror. I was becoming a woman who was unapologetic.

The light turned green and as I drove away; I thought to myself, just like that house, a lot of my self-renovations had been completed. However, there was still a lot to be done. I was still a work in progress.

CHAPTER 13

THIS THING CALLED FORGIVENESS

"Our unhealed wounds are invisible prisons."
—Katherine Woodward Thomas

Forgiveness is hard. I really thought I was maturing in my Christian walk, but one Wednesday night in bible study, my pastor taught a class on forgiveness and I realized I still had a long way to go.

It had been almost two years since my divorce. I was still living with my sister, trying to adjust to life as a single woman. I felt relieved to be out of a toxic relationship. Every day I was learning to surrender my internal doubts and fears to God so I could live this bold life I dreamed about. Through therapy, I was doing the work to heal my mental and spiritual health. I was no longer afraid of the tough questions my therapist would ask. I welcomed the deep and personal conversations we had, because in those conversations I could release my deepest and darkest secrets and fears into the universe, purifying my soul. Prayer became a part of my daily routine. Every chance I could get I was at Barnes & Noble reading and buying books on self-love, empowerment and my favorite biographies about powerful women. I was working out three to four times a week. I was creating a new circle of influence for myself. Cutting off people who I felt did not have my best interest at heart. I was learning to silence the opinions, judgments and distractions of the world, and I was beginning to listen to my own voice. To the outside world, it seemed as though things were looking up for me. And I was good at making it look that way. But on the inside, I was still incensed with rage. I had no financial help from my ex-husband. I found employment with a company as a Real Estate Closer, booking and funding mortgage loans. This job offered great benefits and room for advancement, but I still had to find a part-time job to make ends meet.

I was so stressed about money, and I was really upset that I was not able to afford my own place. There were nights I felt so lonely and just wanted to be held by someone. The struggles of being lonely and feeling penniless fueled the bitterness I carried towards my ex-husband. He had destroyed me emotionally, mentally, and financially. I had given this man twenty-five years of my life, and it angered me that he could be so coldhearted and ruthless towards someone he said he loved. The way he treated me was not love. The only person he loved in the relationship was himself. It infuriated me that he was unable to sit down and divide things out equally in regards to our finances and personal possessions, because I did contribute. Where was all this love he claimed he still had for me, why were we unable to end things amicably without any animosity? Why was he so determined to be so hateful towards me?

From the moment I left, in his narcissist way, my ex-husband made my life a living hell with placing blame, being hurtful and insulting. He fought me about everything from finances to what things I could take from the house. I was only allowed one day to come to the house and pick up things, and when I got there that day, he had already packed what he wanted me to have in a few boxes and I was not allowed to take anything else. He was relentless in trying to destroy my relationship with my sons and with my family, saying things that were untrue about me. He said I was gay, I was having sex with multiple men, including family members. There were the texts where he'd share intimate details about all women he was seeing and how they were satisfying his sexual desires. Then there were the texts about how much he still loved and missed me. Blocking his number was the best thing I ever did. I didn't care if I ever saw him again. How could someone so cold and vicious know love?

Even though it had been almost two years since our divorce a part of me still felt imprisoned by his cruel words. There were days I would be so angry and infuriated without any reason. If I felt threatened or unheard by anyone, I'd attack like a rattlesnake. Doling out consequences and wanting revenge from anyone who I felt hurt me. Then there were days I just wanted to withdraw into a dark, private corner and be all by myself. I'd tell myself I was better off alone. That way, no one was ever going to hurt me again. Over and over, I tried to bury those feelings deep down inside, but it was hard when my sons mentioned my ex-husband's name or when I truly had to face my circumstances. There were nights I laid in bed asking God how to overcome the feelings of brokenness and despair I was experiencing. I wondered if I would ever feel love, joy, peace, or happiness again.

One Saturday in my therapy session, I shared these feelings with my therapist. I also expressed how afraid I was of becoming an angry black woman that I always read about and saw in movies. The woman who was mad at the world and afraid to let people in. I shared that eventually I wanted a relationship with someone who loved me unconditionally, but I was afraid that the resentment I carried inside of me would prevent it. She took a moment to respond, then she kindly asked if I had forgiven my husband, and I immediately corrected her. "You mean ex-husband and yes, I think I have," I said rudely.

In a compassionate and non-threatening way she replied, "I don't think you have."

I took a deep breath, because I could feel myself becoming

annoyed and I was trying to calm down. I sat up straight in my chair and glared back at her. She felt my uneasiness and before I could spit out my words of venom to put her in her place, she wrote down something in her notepad and handed it to me. I took it from her hand, and she politely told me it was best we ended our session early today. She could tell that I was irritated by her comment, so ending the session was probably the best, before I said some things that I would later regret. In my car, I looked at the piece of paper she gave me that I had balled up in my hand. It was a Bible verse Ephesians 4: 31-32. I looked it up on my phone. It read, "**Let all bitterness and wrath and anger and clamor and slander be put away from you along with malice. Be kind to one another, tenderhearted, forgiving one another, as God in Christ forgave you.**" What does this mean I thought? I had forgiven my ex-husband, I said to myself. I threw my phone over in the passenger seat and started my car, turned the music up real loud to block out my thoughts, and drove back to my sister's house. I told myself my therapist had no clue what she was talking about. That night in bed I tossed and turned, still pissed off about my therapy session from earlier that day. I should have told her how I felt about her comment. I asked myself why I kept quiet and as I started to drift off to sleep, I thought maybe it's time to end therapy.

I woke up still mad at my therapist and thinking about the Bible verse she gave me to read. In my prayers, I asked God for guidance on this whole forgiveness thing. My therapist had planted a seed of doubt in my mind. She knew I'd be bothered by what she said and upset about ending our session so abruptly. By giving me that Bible verse, she was gently sharing with me that the unexplained resentment I was harboring had a lot to do with forgiveness.

"I need clarity, God," I said as I ended my prayers and got dressed for church. That Sunday in church, when our pastor called for altar prayer, I went to the altar and again I prayed for guidance and clarity. I wanted answers on forgiveness, so I could release this anger that was eating me up on the inside.

After church, I stopped at Barnes & Noble like I always did and while I was there, I found a book by Max Lucado titled *A Love Worth Giving*. On the back of the cover, it read, "Down to your last dose of forgiveness? You may be holding just the book you need." I saw it as a sign and I bought the book. I started reading it immediately. I was hoping this book would help me understand this thing called forgiveness. Little did I know that God would soon give me all the answers I needed.

That Monday I took the book to work so I could continue reading it. I was trying to gain some sense of clarity on whether I had forgiven my ex. I really wanted to prove my therapist wrong because in my mind, I had forgiven him. By Wednesday, I was half way through the book and from what I had read so far; I was starting to question myself. Maybe my therapist was right. I thought to myself. On my way to Bible study, that evening I decided that I needed to discuss this whole forgiveness thing with my teacher.

Bible study was held every Wednesday night at my church. The classes were set up according to age. In the sanctuary our Senior Pastor held a combined class. I normally attended the young adult class. It was called the young adult class, but the ages varied. Some people were close to my age or older, and some were younger than me. I really liked this class because the teacher taught in a way that allowed us the freedom to ask questions and openly discuss the lesson's topic and how it applied in today's world. We talked about our struggles and our fears. We laughed and cried together, and there was no judgement. What happened in the class stayed in the class. To me, this made it feel intimate and safe. But on this particular Wednesday night, we were informed that our teacher was out sick, so we all made our way to different classes, and I decided to attend the combined class in the sanctuary.

I walked into the sanctuary just as my pastor started to talk. I quickly found a seat. This class was more reserved than the class I normally attended. No one really talked back or asked questions.

Everyone just sat there and listened to what was being taught. Once everyone was seated, my pastor gave us the topic for the lesson. Tonight the lesson would be on forgiveness. *Look at God*, I thought. I opened my book, got a pen out of my purse, and prepared myself to take notes.

My pastor explained how the Bible teaches us that it is in our best interest to forgive. He said that to have the spirit of unforgiveness not only makes us bitter and full of resentment; it complicates our daily walk with God. He asked the class, this question "Do you ever feel angry or bitter and you don't know why?" A bunch of people in the class said "yes" and a lot of us just nodded our heads in agreement. He replied, "You just might be struggling with unforgiveness." He had my full attention when he said this. I went from leaning back in my seat to sitting up straight and I listened closely.

He continued to explain that forgiving someone doesn't mean we are condoning the other person's behavior, but by forgiving, we are reclaiming power over our lives. He asked more questions, *"How many of you can truly say you have forgiven someone who has hurt you?"* We all raised our hands. Then he asked, *"Do you still have a difficult time being in the same room or being around that person?"* I wrote yes in my notes. *"Do you become uneasy every time you hear that person's name?"* Again, I wrote yes in my notes. Pastor continued, *"If you answered yes to these questions, can you truly say you have forgiven them for the pain they caused you?"* Then he smiled and said in a thunderous voice, *"No, you have not truly forgiven."*

When I heard him say this, I became agitated and my mind became filled with questions. *"How do you forgive someone who continues to hurt you over and over? And why should I keep subjecting myself to hurtful behavior"* But I didn't say a word, because in that moment, I could feel the rage rising up inside of me, and if I opened my mouth and said one word, I would not be able to hold back what I call my anger tears. So, I sat there in silence and listened while my insides boiled. But I was not the only person who was affected by what he said because the whole class was in an uproar. People started to engage with their questions and concerns.

"Just because I don't want to be around someone who has hurt me, doesn't mean I haven't forgiven them," I heard a woman say.

"But shouldn't we protect our hearts?" I heard someone else say. Then a man in the class said, "Hurt me once shame on you, hurt me twice shame on me. There won't be a third time." Everyone in the class started to laugh and nod our heads in agreement.

My pastor started to respond to all the questions everyone was asking. I listened closely to his answers to each question. In one response, he explained that we have to commit to letting go. He explained that forgiveness will not happen in a second or even in a day, but we have to allow peace to enter. The more I listened, it became clear to me that the anger and the bitterness I felt inside was due to the unforgiveness I carried. The more I listened, I realized it was time for me to figure out how to let go and shake off this chain of unforgiveness, if I wanted to experience real and true peace. As my pastor continued to teach, I took very detailed notes so I could refer back and study them more when I was alone. Before class ended, he explained to the class that God is very clear about forgiveness. He referred to Ephesians 4:32, **"Be kind to one another tenderhearted, forgiving one another as God in Christ forgives you."** This was the same scripture my therapist had given me in our last session. The last point my pastor made was that if you are struggling with unforgiveness, you need to find a way to resolve it, let it go, forgive and forget.

After class that night, I left in a hurry. I didn't stay around and talk like I normally did. I hurried to my car and once inside my anger, tears started to flow. The last thing I wanted to do was to forget. I was never going to allow myself to be held captive to someone else's demands or requests. The years of constant pleasing and pretending and the fear of saying *no* were over. In my mind if I forgot; it was like accepting what had happened to me. While I drove to my sister's house, I kept asking myself, *How do I forgive and forget?*

That night in my room, as I laid in bed, I started to think about all the anger and bitterness I carried inside of me. I was bitter that my father never showed me his love. He never took the time to know me or accept me. I was angry at my mother for all the times I felt she took her frustrations out on me. I was troubled over things that had happened to me in my marriage. I thought I would be married to this man forever. Yes, he was an excellent provider, and at times, he really made me happy. But my ex-husband was in a constant battle with himself when it came to showing me love. Repeatedly, he took his frustrations out on me. The drinking, the physical abuse, the verbal outbursts and endless gas-lighting always left me traumatized, defeated, feeling unloved and emotionally burned out. Laying there in bed that night, reminiscing over my life, it became transparent that I had been carrying so much discontentment inside me. It was crystal clear that if I could remember all of my past hurts, then I have never truly forgiven anyone, and my unwillingness to forgive had left me unhinged emotionally and spiritually for years. But tonight, in that bible study, I learned what true forgiveness should look like.

That Thursday, while on my lunch break, I continued to read <u>A Love Worth Giving</u> by Max Lucado. I was up to Chapter 9, "The Heart Full of Hurts." As I read this chapter, the author said something that stood out to me. He said, *"Can you list the times God has forgiven you?"* He went on to say, *"You didn't deserve to be hurt by the people who hurt you, but neither did you deserve to be forgiven by God."* I thought about what I read the rest of the day. I thought about what I learned that night before in Bible Study. I re-read Ephesians 4:31-32. the scripture my therapist gave me, and the scripture my pastor closed out class with. After reading this Bible verse again, I found myself dwelling on past hurts and my inability to forgive, let go and forget. Later that evening, I continued to read and the author asked, *"Do you think God could heal your angry heart?",* "Do you want Him to?" I answered "yes". I wanted God to heal my angry heart.

Once I finished this book, I bought more books on forgiveness. In my daily prayers, I asked God for guidance. In my therapy sessions, I was more open to hear what my therapist had to say about forgiveness. I reached out to my mentors and asked for advice. One of my mentors suggested that I do some soul searching to try to figure out where the anger and bitterness began. So that's what I did. I read through my journals, which overflowed with stories from my past. In particular, there was one entry where I wrote about how I wished I had known my father, who was now deceased. As I read that entry, I shared how I yearned for his love, his approval, and protection. I wrote about how hurt I felt to know he had other kids that he accepted, but he never accepted me. In another entry, I wrote about how I felt as though my mother was angry at my dad, for his absence in our life, and how I felt she took that anger out on me. The more I read those entries, I realized that was where it all began for me. This is when I started to feel unworthy and unloved. This is where I started to hold resentment and bitterness. I decided this was where my road of true forgiveness would begin.

My first step was to make peace with my dad. Even though he was deceased, I needed to resolve the feelings of abandonment I had towards him. After much thought and some research, I found an article online titled "Dear Love, Healing Through Writing." The author of this article had a similar story to mine. She was carrying some unresolved issues with a family member who was now deceased and her therapist suggested that she write this person a letter sharing how she felt. At first, she thought it was stupid, but once she did it, she felt so relieved. After reading this article, I decided I would try this approach. I would write my dad a letter.

In that letter, I wrote about how I felt abandoned and unloved by him. I wrote about how I wondered if he ever thought about me, because I thought about him. I knew he would never read the letter, but it felt good to write those things down and get them out of my head and out of my thoughts. His refusal to know me confused me as a child, and it still confused me as an adult. Through therapy, when I had to discuss my childhood, I learned that not knowing my dad caused extreme abandonment issues for me. Him not being a part of my life had a lot to do with my low self-worth and why I struggled with relationships, especially with men. Once I finished the letter, I read it over and over for about an hour. Then I folded it up and put it in my purse. There were days when I read this letter I'd cry uncontrollably. Then there were days when I read it. I'd become angry and cuss him out. But the more I read that letter, the more relieved I felt. I was no longer carrying around ill feelings for him. I had brought all those feelings to the surface. I had taken ownership. I had taken back my power. This began the process of self-forgiveness and healing. I kept the letter for about a month, reading it periodically. Then one day I ripped it up and threw it away. I had forgiven, and I was ready to forget and let go.

Next on my list, I needed to forgive my mother. She was a teenage mother doing the best she knew how to do. And through therapy, I learned that she was probably dealing with some unresolved issues from her past that I knew nothing about. Those issues most likely had a lot to do with why she was so mean and angry all the time. Now that she was older, I noticed that my mother had become a lot calmer and she seemed happy with her life. She was active in her church. She had friends that she hung out with, and she was married. So, it was time for me to stop being bitter and mend our relationship. It was time to take ownership of my behavior and move forward. To let go and forgive.

I started to make a conscious effect, to include her in my life. I would invite her to go with me to places, and when I traveled to visit my sons and their families, I'd asked her if she wanted to go. I made a genuine effort to no longer see her as the person I remembered her to be, and to see her as the person she had become. Our relationship was still a work in progress, but I knew that in her own way, she loved me. Forgiving, my mother and my dad were only the beginning. As I continued to work through the process of forgiving, letting go and forgetting, I soon realized it was time for me to figure out how to truly forgive myself. For most of my life, I had been in survival mode. I pretended that my past hadn't affected me. But really it had. It had taken up a lot of my mental thoughts. It had disabled me from being free in my mind and in my spirit. In my mind, some part of me still believed that I deserved all the bad things that happened to me.

During one of my therapy sessions, I shared with my therapist what I had been doing and she was excited to hear what I was doing. She asked me how I was feeling about the whole process. I shared that I felt relief, but I was still struggling to forgive myself and my ex-husband. I shared that I needed to figure this forgiveness thing out, if I wanted to be a perfect Christian, or what I thought was the perfect Christian. My therapist shared with me that there are no perfect Christians. She then explained that in order for me to have authentic healing and to make peace with my past shame and hurts I needed to forgive myself and let go. *"But how do I forgive myself?"* I asked.

My therapist explained that one way to let go was to not be afraid to share my story. It was good that I was able to write down my thoughts, but I needed to be okay with talking about my past. Sharing my story would give me power. She shared that being transparent was very freeing.

"Authenticity is the ultimate act of showing yourself love," she said with a smile. "Another way is to realize you're not perfect, and it is okay to be flawed. Your imperfections make you who you are. They tell your story and your story is significant."

I left that session feeling kind of torn. One part of me was on cloud nine from all the positive feedback. However, the other part of me was afraid to share my past. The last person I opened up to was my ex-husband and he used my intimate thoughts, fears and insecurities against me. Sharing my story meant that I'd be opening myself up to the opinions and judgement of others. Sharing my story meant that I would be opening a door that I so desperately wanted to stay closed. That night, I wrote in my journal about how determined I was to cleanse myself of all the bitterness inside of me. I had written a letter to my Dad. I was working on my relationship with my mother, and I was doing the work to forgive and love myself. As I wrote, I could feel the weight of the unforgiveness chains becoming lighter.

That following Saturday in my therapy session, we talked more about forgiveness. I shared how I was making a conscious effort to work on my relationship with my mother, and we talked about what I was doing to forgive myself. I shared how I had posted affirmations around my room about forgiveness, self-love, and self-worth to encourage myself. When my therapist asked if I still had an uneasy feeling about sharing my story, I explained that I wasn't ready to handle the judgement of others. She made it very clear that to truly forgive myself, I had to come clean. I had to rip the bandage off of the wound so it could heal properly. The longer I continued to cover and protect, the longer it would take for me to find my authentic self. Then the topic came up about my ex-husband and as soon as I heard his name, I could feel my stomach start to turn and my mood change. I became agitated, silent and the anger tears started to flow. I despised him. I was not ready to forgive him. All I could think about was how much I wanted to retaliate. I wanted him to hurt.

Sitting there, I thought about how eager I always was to please him. How I had given him every ounce of me: my heart, my soul, and my friendship. I had loved him unconditionally, but his love for me always came with stipulations. My therapist saw how uncomfortable I became. She reminded me that true forgiveness did not make the person who hurt you whole and clean. True forgiveness was about making you whole and clean. She reminded me that faux forgiveness prohibits your spiritual growth and leaves you bound to the hurt. Then she read Matthew 6:14-15, **"If you forgive those who sin against you, your heavenly Father will forgive you. But if you refuse to forgive others, your Father will not forgive your sins."** She walked over, gave me a hug, and told me our time was up. I left that session pissed. I knew I had to forgive him, but I wasn't ready. I knew it was going to take a lot of work for me to forgive my ex-husband. I wasn't sure if I could totally commit to doing the work. I was thankful that

God had delivered me out of a dysfunctional marriage, but as long as I was unwilling to forgive my ex-husband and let go, I would always still be a victim and not a victor.

Over the next month and after a lot of praying, and a few more therapy sessions, and with my therapist's persuasion, I finally decided to change the way I thought about my ex-husband. I was determined to master this thing called forgiveness. I wanted to be totally free of his control. I started to only think about the good times I had in my marriage instead of only thinking about the bad times. In my prayers, I prayed for him and for his well being. When my sons mentioned his name, instead of allowing the anger to rise up inside of me, I would exhale and take deep breaths and release it out into the universe.

The more I went to therapy, the more I surrendered and talked about the deep feelings that were buried so deep inside of me, the better I felt. Over time, I could see myself becoming more vulnerable, holding nothing back. The chains of unforgiveness kept getting lighter and lighter. I noticed my mood changing. I no longer thought about all the things I should have done differently in my life or in my marriage. I was still not ready to be around my ex-husband, but I no longer held contentment for him in my heart. My relationship with my mother had begun to heal, and I was no longer angry at my dad. I finally started to accept my imperfections, and live in my truth. This way of living made me feel courageous, brave, bold, and vulnerable. Through my pastor, my therapist, and my circle, God was teaching me the art of forgiveness. I still have a lot to learn, but I now have a peace within that I never felt before and my heart is no longer heavy.

CHAPTER 14

BRAND NEW ME

*"Imagine the best version of yourself
and show up every day as her"*

– UNKNOWN

After fighting traffic and getting lost, I finally found the studio. As I parked my car, I saw my friend standing at the entrance of the building waiting for me with a big smile on her face. As I got closer to the building, my whole body became electrified with excitement. I followed my friend up the stairs into a big room. Once we were inside, I couldn't help but smile as I thought, *How did I get talked into this?*

Tonight I was attending my first pole dance class. I walked to a corner in the room to drop my gym bag and I glanced at the poles perfectly spaced out, reaching from the floor to the ceiling. The flashing strobe lights set the mood in the room, surrounded by mirrored walls. I noticed that some of the ladies were wearing six-inch heels with sports bras and booty shorts. While the rest of us, *"the newbies"*, had on t-shirts, shorts or leggings. I saw that some of the ladies were barefooted, so I sat on the floor to remove my shoes as well. As I started to stand back up, a tall, muscular woman with a long ponytail, wearing six-inch heels and a headset, walked past me and announced we had five minutes. My friend let me know that she was our instructor and to hurry up and find a pole. Feeling nervous and bewildered, I walked over to a pole next to her. The friend who invited me was someone I trained with in my Krav Maga class. She was always talking about how much she enjoyed pole dancing and how it was a good workout, and how the class gave her a liberated feeling after each class. I was not sure if it was for me, but after much persuasion, I decided to go with her. Besides, I was curious about the whole pole dance experience.

After the five minutes were up, the instructor walked over to her pole and got into position. Dance for You, by Beyoncé, started to play through the speakers, and our instructor commenced into her routine. I watched as she cascaded up and down her pole, all while twirling, flipping, and grinding. I was in awe. She made it look so elegant and effortless. She was so comfortable in her skin. Her confidence overpowered the room. My friend could sense my uneasiness and she whispered to me, "don't worry, you got this."

I just smiled and replied, "Yeah, I am not going to be doing any of that."

Once she finished, she instructed us to stretch and warm-up. While I was stretching, a feeling of newness came over me. The old me would have never done anything like this. After we stretched, we were told to get comfortable, lose our inhibition and relax. A couple of the experienced dancers, along with the instructor, took the first three poles in the front of the room and embarked on showing us the basic moves we were to learn on this night.

When they were done one of them said "okay ladies grab your pole." Then she said, "If you can dance you can pole dance."

Another dancer instructed us to close our eyes and take a deep breath in. Then she told us to open our eyes immediately when the music started. I closed my eyes, took a deep breath and listened for the music. A few seconds later I heard Rihanna's song "Work" come full blast through the speakers. I opened my eyes, grabbed my pole, and started imitating the moves. This was the perfect song, I thought as I began swaying to the music. I focused my eyes on the lead dancers as they guided us through the moves. I looked over at my friend and we both smiled at each other as she took hold of her pole and started dancing. This wasn't her first class, so the moves came easy to her, but for me it took a lot more effort. I continued to vibe with the music and before I knew it, I was keeping up with the instructor. My moves weren't perfect, but as I checked myself out in the mirror, I looked pretty good. Who knew?

The whole session lasted for an hour, and once it ended, the instructor came and asked me what I thought about the whole experience. Feeling exhilarated and free, I admitted to her that I was hooked. I felt empowered, and for the first time in a long time, I felt comfortable in my skin. I shared with her that it had been a long time since I saw myself this way. I felt SEXY! We both laughed when I told her I needed to buy me some six-inch heels before the next class, but no booty shorts, because I wasn't there yet. That night, as I drove home, I couldn't stop smiling. I LOVED the way that class made me feel, and I was so proud of myself for stepping out of my comfort zone.

It was now 2017. I had been divorced for about four years, and I had grown a lot. Through therapy, church, and my circle of influence, I had learned how to deal with my inner demons. I started a journey of discovery and over the course of this adventure; I had become a brand-new person. I was no longer embarrassed of my past. In those four years, I had dismantled the person I thought others wanted me to be, and for the first time in my life I didn't see myself as the confused, broken little girl who was constantly pleasing, pretending, and looking for acceptance. The brand new me believed everything I needed was already inside of me. I learned to turn inward, to listen to my own voice and to trust myself. I removed the external distractions and opinions of the world. In the mirror, I saw a woman who was learning to show herself love, who finally knew her worth and wasn't afraid to walk in her uniqueness. Each passing day I felt liberated, free-spirited and courageous. With all this new confidence, I thought that maybe I was ready to date and be in a relationship. But I quickly changed my mind when I found myself dating Mr. Narcissistic.

I met what I thought was a very intelligent and interesting man one weekend, while working at my part-time job as a hostess. He was an older man, in his late fifties, and very distinguished. He seemed nice and instantly when I saw him; I wanted to get to know him. He came into the restaurant a few more times for dinner and one Saturday while he was leaving, he handed me his business card. I don't know if this was a new thing that men were doing, but normally when a man gave me a business card, I tore it up and threw it in the trash, but this time I kept his card. After a couple of weeks of soul searching, I finally talked myself into sending him a text message. In the message, I told him who I was and asked if he was still interested in getting to know me. He called me the next day.

Our first conversation was pleasant. We discussed our ages, our careers, our hobbies and how many kids we each had. It was a short conversation and after we hung up, I looked forward to our next one. Since I worked on the weekends, we planned that once I got off, we would meet up for a late dinner. This was the first man I dated since my divorce, and I was scared and guarded. He was charming and I enjoyed the company, so I told myself that I needed to put my fears aside, calm down and try to connect.

We met for an enjoyable dinner the following Friday at a Moroccan restaurant. Again, the conversation was good-natured. There was a lot of laughter and I found out we had some of the same views on life. When it was over, he walked me to my car and we said our goodbyes. Later that night, he called me to check and see if I made it home and to express how he enjoyed the evening.

Things were going well for about a month. I looked forward to his phone calls and seeing him on the weekends. But the more time I spent with him and the more we talked on the phone, I started to feel uneasy, like something wasn't right. I don't know why I felt this way, but the feeling was there and it would not go away. The more we saw each other, the stronger this feeling was.

The main thing I learned from therapy was to pay close attention to restless and unsettled feelings and not be afraid to act on them. So I made a conscious effort to see past the persona he portrayed. I wanted to see the genuine person. Soon I started to notice things about him that seemed familiar to me. He always needed to be right and in control of everything. We had to eat where he wanted to eat; he always found something wrong with the places I suggested. He'd make these little sarcastic remarks that left me feeling inferior and belittled. He was overly self-involved and vain, always quick to point out my imperfections. My views and opinions were secondary to his. He always made it known how smart he was and he bragged continuously about his college degrees. Then there were the times he wanted to counsel me on how I was supposed to feel about things, or how I should feel about him. He truly had a superiority complex, always trying to impress me with gifts and expensive dinners.

The more the relationship progressed, I noticed that he was very insecure. He had this exaggerated need for attention and validation. Always worrying about his image. It was all he talked about. He lacked empathy. Every conversation always ended up being about him, how successful he was, and how much money he had. He'd become upset when I couldn't spend time with him. Over and over he tried to invite himself to my family gatherings, and eventually he started showing up at my hostess job unexpectedly. Then there were the late-night calls, where he wanted to talk all night, and he'd become upset when I didn't want to. On top of the phone calls, he'd text me early in the morning and through-out the day. His constant need for recognition and not respecting my boundaries became intrusive. His possessive behavior left me feeling caged, and I couldn't breathe.

Eventually I regretted the day I met him. Then one night while talking on the phone, I expressed my uneasiness, and how I felt like he was not respecting me. I went on to say that I think we should take a break. I explained that I didn't feel like this relationship was going to work. I told him maybe it's still too soon for me, and I was not ready for the type of relationship he was looking for. I shared how we had only been dating for a few months and I felt caged by his constant need for us to be together all the time. There was a brief silence, then he went into counselor mode, analyzing everything I said, twisting my words and telling me that was not how I really felt. I was just trying to sabotage our relationship.

I instantly became defensive. I rose up in the bed, and in true angry black woman mode, I cut him off. I began yelling through the phone, letting him know that what I said was exactly how I felt. My thoughts were very clear, precise and on point. Then, before I hung up on him, I told him I was done with him, his ego and this relationship. Who the hell was he to tell me how I felt? In that moment after I hung up, a big smile came over my face and I started laughing out loud uncontrollably. A feeling of exhilaration came over me. In that moment, I realized that I was definitely not the same woman I once was. The old me would have just sat there and listened to everything Mr. Narcissistic said. Analyzing his every word. Then I would have spent the rest of the night convincing myself to conform to the person he thought I should be. But not today. I held my ground and stayed true to my inner voice. It was a brand new day, and I was a brand new woman.

The more I thought about the relationship, I realized why I always felt uncomfortable around Mr. Narcissistic. He had the same dogmatic personality as my ex-husband. He had the same God complex, and I was walking right back into the environment I had left. I grabbed my journal and wrote the following question: "Is this the type of person I was attracting?" Then I questioned why I didn't trust my first instinct. Why did I continue in a relationship when something inside of me was telling me something was not right? For the next hour, I stared at those questions and as my eyes became heavy, I told myself that until I could answer those questions, I was not going to date anyone.

Not knowing the answers to those questions scared me. Because if I couldn't answer them, my fear was I would revert back to that woman I had fought so hard to restore.

Mr. Narcissistic reached out to me a few more times after that night, and each time we spoke, I explained to him that the way I felt had not changed. I was not interested in having a relationship or a friendship with him, and each time he tried to convince me I was wrong. In one conversation, he expressed that he knew he was the perfect man for me, but I knew he wasn't. The woman I was becoming needed to be in a relationship where I could breathe. I needed to be with someone who would see me as their partner, their equal. I needed to know that I would be heard and not ignored. I wanted to be in a relationship with someone who respected my boundaries. I wanted a man who loved me and all my flaws. Mr. Narcissistic was incapable of being that person, so after our last conversation, I blocked his number.

In September of that same year, I moved into my very own place. I had watched some apartments being built for months down the street from my part-time job, and once they were completed, I left work early one day to check them out. I knew my budget, so at first I was a little hesitant to view the model because the rent was high. I didn't know if I could afford it, but something inside of me said "go ahead and take the tour."

I viewed a two bedroom apartment, which was too large for me. Then a studio, which I felt was too small. The moment I walked into the one bedroom apartment, a peaceful feeling came over me and the voice inside of me let me know it was the right place for me. When I walked through the front door, I walked right into the kitchen, which opened up to a small sitting area. The kitchen had a huge breakfast bar with a lot of cabinets, and to the left, there was a built-in desk with bookshelves above it. The sitting area was small, but it had large windows that open out onto a balcony. The bedroom was a nice size and it had a large window along one of the walls, and the bathroom was large with a long countertop with lots of storage and a mirror that covered most of the wall. There was also a huge walk-in closet with built-in shelves. I told the leasing agent this is the one I wanted and I signed the lease that day.

A couple of weeks later I moved in. I filled my apartment with love. I decorated it with all the things I liked. I made sure to place all my favorite poems and quotes in places where I could see them. I placed pictures of my sons, my grandkids, and my family everywhere. My favorite color purple was everywhere, and I decorated the bathroom in total white because I always wanted an all-white bathroom. All of my books filled the built-in bookshelves. I bought plants to add life. That night in bed, I cried tears of joy. This was my first place as the woman I had worked so hard to create. Even though my finances were tight, it felt good to be in my own space, filled with all the things I loved. Each day I woke up and I let God know how grateful and thankful I was. A joyous feeling came over me each time I walked into my apartment, because I knew I was walking into a place of calmness. I posted a quote right at the entrance as I walked in that read, *"Be aware of the energy you bring into this space"* to remind me that whatever mess I was dealing without outside these four walls was not allowed to enter my home. I felt free and I enjoyed the tranquility. I hadn't felt this way in a long time and each day I looked forward to coming home.

One Wednesday after bible study, I got into a deep discussion with a family member from church and we decided to go grab some dinner after class. While we ate dinner, she asked me about my dating status. I told her I didn't have one and was in no hurry to get one. I explained that eventually it would be great to be with someone, but for now, I was perfectly content being alone. I was in no rush. We both laughed. I shared that in my next relationship I wanted to be with a man that would help me grow while loving me for who I was. He'd understand me and support my dreams. He'd feed my intellect and not belittle me. He would not be afraid to be transparent. He wouldn't need alcohol or his ego stroked to prove his manhood. She said, "Amen to that," while we high-fived each other. I told her I wanted a man who was confident in who he was and comfortable in his own skin. We'd have a lot of deep conversations and there would be a lot of laughter. Showing affection would not be a problem for him, and whenever he'd hold me in his arms, I would feel safe and secure. Our sex life would be breathtaking and mind blowing, leaving little to the imagination. My sista-friend laughed and replied, "Good luck with that".

I laughed and said, *"A girl can dream."* My last requirement was the most important one, God had to be first in his life. We had to share the same beliefs.

After dinner and as I drove home, I thought more about our conversation. I thought about one of my favorite books in the bible. The book of Joshua. Joshua had fearless faith. He was a strong, bold, and a fierce leader who trusted and believed in God. I wanted the man in my next relationship to have attributes like Joshua. I knew I was asking God for a lot, but these were the characteristics I was looking for. Until I met that person, I was okay being alone. Being alone to me was far better than being made to feel unimportant and invisible. I never wanted to feel that way again.

The most important life lesson I had learned on this journey was that my life and my happiness were my responsibility, not anyone else's. I deserved to have a relationship filled with love. A love that wasn't determined by material things but a love that was selfless. I was not going to settle.

One evening while out for my run, I started to think about how far I had come. I thought about how I came to terms and accepted responsibility for the chaos in my life. I thought about how if I had stayed in my marriage being a cowardly woman; I was blocking my destiny. I could not become the woman I dreamed of becoming. By doing the work, I learned the things that happened in my marriage were just as much my fault. I should have fought more for myself and for the woman that was screaming to get out. The woman I was becoming had taken self-ownership for her life. The seed of worthlessness that was so deeply planted inside of me had been destroyed. On this journey I learned to not be afraid to ask myself the hard questions, and I didn't have a problem reexamining my thoughts if needed. I understood that my ex-husband's issues were his issues and not mine. But it was my responsibility to figure out if I wanted to continue to stay in an abusive relationship. People thought I had lost my mind when I left. They told me I was crazy to leave that big home and financial security, but all I could think about was how broken, empty and hopeless I felt. I knew if I had stayed any longer, I would have eventually committed suicide to relieve the pain I felt inside. Love should never be hurtful and tear you down. Love should never have contingencies. My whole life had been filled with contingencies and boundaries from others who claimed to love me. This is how they controlled me. But I now knew that wasn't love.

I thought about how I had developed an ongoing relationship with God. I had known of God most of my life, but finally, I could say I knew Him personally. We talked regularly. He was my running partner. I called Him ABBA. There was nothing I could not share with Him. He had shown me what real love looked like by loving me unconditionally. His love for me had made me fierce and fearless. His love taught me that I am worthy of all the blessings I received in this life. I am not perfect, my life is not perfect, but who has the perfect life? There will be times I will struggle with insecurities of the unknown, and that is okay. I now understand that at times, I'll still become anxious with the challenges of this world, but instead of turning outward to others for answers and instead of looking for peace in temporal things, I will look inward and to God for guidance. I am happy with the life I am creating. Back at my apartment as I undressed to get into the shower, I stared at myself in the mirror and started to sing Alicia Keys' song "Brand New Me." My favorite part is the chorus *"It's been a while, I'm not who I was before. You look surprised. Your words don't burn me anymore, been meaning to tell you, but I guess it's clear to see, don't be mad, it's just the brand-new kind of me."*

I had finally found peace.

www.ingramcontent.com/pod-product-compliance
Lightning Source LLC
Chambersburg PA
CBHW072007290426
44109CB00018B/2167